Edexcel GCSE

History B

Schools History Project

Crime and punishment (Option 1B) and Protest, law and order in the twentieth century (Option 3B)

Allan Todd   Martyn Whittock
Series editor: Angela Leonard

A PEARSON COMPANY

Published by Pearson Education Limited, a company incorporated in England and Wales, having its registered office at Edinburgh Gate, Harlow, Essex, CM20 2JE. Registered company number: 872828

www.pearsonschoolsandfecolleges.co.uk

Edexcel is a registered trademark of Edexcel Limited

Text © Pearson Education Limited 2009
First published 2009

12 11 10 09
10 9 8 7 6 5 4 3 2 1

British Library Cataloguing in Publication Data
A catalogue record for this book is available from the British Library.

ISBN 978 1 846904 41 7

Edited by Florence Production Ltd, Stoodleigh, Devon
Typeset by HL Studios, Long Hanborough, Oxford
Original illustrations © Pearson Education Limited 2009
Cover design by Pearson Education Limited
Picture research by Susi Paz
Cover photo/illustration © Alamy/Classic Image
Printed in Spain by Graficas Estella

Websites
There are links to relevant websites in this book. In order to ensure that the links are up to date, that the links work, and that the sites are not inadvertently linked to sites that could be considered offensive, we have made the links available on the Heinemann website at www.heinemann.co.uk/hotlinks. When you access the site, the express code is 4417P.

Disclaimer
This material has been published on behalf of Edexcel and offers high-quality support for the delivery of Edexcel qualifications.

This does not mean that the material is essential to achieve any Edexcel qualification, nor does it mean that it is the only suitable material available to support any Edexcel qualification. Edexcel material will not be used verbatim in setting any Edexcel examination or assessment. Any resource lists produced by Edexcel shall include this and other appropriate resources.

Copies of official specifications for all Edexcel qualifications may be found on the Edexcel website: www.edexcel.com

Acknowledgements

The author and publisher would like to thank the following individuals and organisations for permission to reproduce the following material:

Photographs

akg-images pp. 53, 58, 68, 87, 99, 117; Alamy/The Print Collector pp. 95, 111; Alamy/Martin Jenkinson pp. 135, 136; Alamy?/Mary Evans Picture Library pp. 106, 108, 112, 132, 152; Alamy/Select Images p. 42; Alamy/Trinity Mirror/Mirrorpix p. 108; The Art Archive/Archaeological Museum El-Jem Tunisia/Gianni Dagli Orti p. 57; The Bridgeman Art Library/© Lambeth Palace Library, London, UK p. 10, 80; The Bridgeman Art Library/Biblioteque Nationale, Paris, France p. 4; The Bridgeman Art Library/British Library, London, UK/© British Library Board. All Rights Reserved pp. 30, 65; The Bridgeman Art Library/British Museum, London, UK p. 20; The Bridgeman Art Library/Fitzwilliam Museum, University of Cambridge, UK pp. 3, 22; The Bridgeman Art Library/Guildhall Library, City of London p. 14; The Bridgeman Art Library/Inner Temple, London, UK pp. 6, 70; The Bridgeman Art Library/Museum of London, UK p. 116; The Bridgeman Art Library/Private Collection pp. 8, 16; The Bridgeman Art Library/Private Collection © Look and Learn p. 20; The Bridgeman Art Library/Private Collection/Ken Walsh p. 14; The Bridgeman Art Library/Private Collection/Roger-Viollet, Paris p. 25; The Bridgeman Art Library/Private Collection/The Stapleton Collection pp. 19, 29, 63; The Bridgeman Art Library/Private Collection/ pp. 81, 85; British Cartoon Archive, University of Kent/Michael Heath published in the Mail on Sunday on the 15th September 2002 p. 38; British Library p. 61; Broughton Inverleith Anti Poll Tax Group p. 145; Corbis/Bettman pp. 105, 110; Daily Express p. 36; EyeVine/Gary Clarkson pp. 143, 161; Fife Council Libraries and Museums p. 138; Fife Mining Museum p. 137; Getty Images/FoxPhotos p. 122; Getty Images/Frederick R.Bunt p. 81; Getty Images/Hulton Archive p. 121; Getty Images/Popperfoto pp. 109, 160; Getty Images/Steve Eason pp. 144, 146, 147, 150, 161; Getty Images/TimeLifePictures p. 114; Imperial War Museum pp. 89, 92, 99; Leon Khun pp. 148, 153; Mark Simmons p. 105; Mary Evans Picture Library pp. 3, 14, 17, 22, 26, 42, 59, 67, 81, 82, 91, 94, 99; The Master and Fellows of Corpus Christi College, Cambridge p. 53; MetPolice p. 44; Mirrorpix/People p. 149; Museum of London p. 24; National Archives pp. 32, 33; PA Photos pp. 3, 122, 147; Punch pp. 31, 120, 123; ReportDigital.co.uk/John Harris pp. 105, 132, 134, 140, 141, 159; ReportDigital.co.uk/John Sturrock pp. 131, 138, 139, 140, 152; Rex Features/Nils Jorgensen p. 130; The Sun Newspaper 09.04.1984 p. 133; Topfoto/World History Archive p. 125; TUC Library Collection, London Metropolitan University pp. 118, 152; www.cartoonstock.com/Mike Baldwin p. 44; www.csiss.org p. 19; www.womensaid.org.uk/Maureen Storey pp. 97, 99.

Written sources

Source D, p. 31, Martin J.Wiener, Men of Blood, CUP, 2004, pp. 11–12; Source E, p. 31, reproduced by kind permission of Continuum International Publishing Group, Clive Emsley, *Hard Men: The English and Violence Since 1750*, Continuum International Publishing Group, 2005, p. 19; Source C, p. 91, parliamentary material is reproduced with the permission of the Controller of HMSO on behalf of Parliament, *Hansard*, HC Deb, 04 & 05 July 1917, vol. 95, cc. 1084 & 1305-6W; Source A, p. 134, quoted in *British Political Opinion 1937-2000: The Gallup Polls* ed. Anthony King, compiled by R.J. Wybrow, 2001, Politico's Publishing, p. 337; Source B, p. 149, an extract from an article in the *Evening Standard*, April 1990; Source B, p.151, Copyright Guardian News and Media Ltd 1991.

Written sources have been freely adapted to make them more accessible for students.

Every effort has been made to contact copyright holders of material reproduced in this book. Any omissions will be rectified in subsequent printings if notice is given to the publishers.

Dedication

For Roy Brown, a good friend in Church work and history discussions (formerly Police Sergeant, Devon and Cornwall Constabulary). From Martyn.

Contents

Option 1B: Crime and punishment

Crime and punishment c1450–c1750

Crime and punishment c1750–c1900

Crime and punishment c1900 to present day

Crime and punishment from Roman Britain to c1450

Welcome to this Edexcel GCSE History B: Schools History Project Resource

Option 1B: Crime and punishment and Option 3B: Protest, law and order in the twentieth century

These resources have been written to fully support Edexcel's new GCSE History B: Schools History Project redeveloped specification. This specification has a focus on change and development through studies of societies in depth and of key themes over time. Written by experienced examiners and packed with exam tips and activities, the book includes lots of engaging features to enthuse students and provide the range of support needed to make teaching and learning a success for all ability levels.

Features of this book

- Learning outcomes structure learning at the start of each topic.

- FASCINATING FACTS give learning extra depth.

- Key words are highlighted in bold on their first occurence in the text. Definitions are in the glossary (see pages 168–169).

- A topic Summary captures the main learning points.

- Before... and After...
  These give information about what has happened before and after the period studied to help you piece everything together.

- Activities Activities provide stimulating tasks for the classroom and homework.

How to use this book

Edexcel GCSE History B: Schools History Project Crime and punishment is divided into the two units that match the specification. Unit 1 begins with the Core Content which all students have to cover, followed by the two Extension Studies, of which students need to answer questions on one. At the end of each section of Core Content (pages 16–17, 30–31 and 44–45) there is a spread devoted to source skills. This has been designed for those studying option 3D The work of the historian but will help all students build up source skills and analysis. Unit 3 contains guidance, instruction and practice questions on the source requirements for the exam.

 A dedicated suite of revision resources for complete exam success. We've broken down the six stages of revision to ensure that you are prepared every step of the way.

 How to get into the perfect 'zone' for your revision.

 Tips and advice on how to effectively plan your revision.

 A checklist of things you should know, revision activities and practice exam questions at the end of each section plus additional exam practice at the end of the book.

 Last-minute advice for just before the exam.

 An overview of what you will have to do in the exam, plus a chance to see what a real exam paper will look like.

 What do you do after your exam? This section contains information on how to get your results and answers to frequently asked questions on what to do next.

ResultsPlus

These features are based on how students have performed in past exams. They are combined with expert advice and guidance from examiners to show you how to achieve better results.

There are four different types of ResultsPlus features throughout this book:

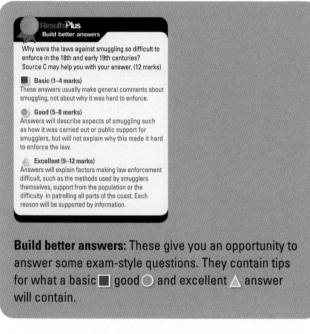

Build better answers: These give you an opportunity to answer some exam-style questions. They contain tips for what a basic ■ good ○ and excellent △ answer will contain.

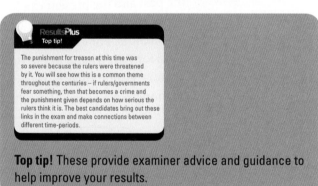

Top tip! These provide examiner advice and guidance to help improve your results.

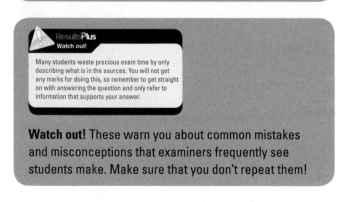

Watch out! These warn you about common mistakes and misconceptions that examiners frequently see students make. Make sure that you don't repeat them!

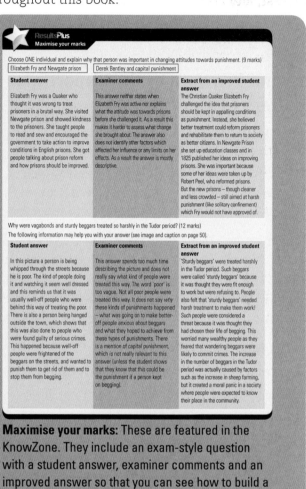

Maximise your marks: These are featured in the KnowZone. They include an exam-style question with a student answer, examiner comments and an improved answer so that you can see how to build a better response.

Crime and punishment

Introduction

Everyone is aware of the importance of crime and punishment. It matters to all of us.

We all have opinions about what should be defined as 'crime' and how it should be prevented – and punished when it happens. Ideas about crime affect what we can and cannot lawfully do. It affects how safe we are and how safe we feel. However, ideas about what 'crime' is (and how to prevent it and punish it) change over time. These changes are often linked to bigger changes happening in society, as well as to the impact of individual people.

In order to explore these changes, we need to look at some of the key periods of British history since 1450. We need to see how crime and punishment has developed and changed in these periods of time. In this way we can get a better idea of both why some things change and why some things remain the same, and what changes have occurred.

Aims and outcomes

By the end of this section you should be able to understand:

- why definitions of 'crime' change over time
- what the causes of crime are, and how these causes differ in different time periods
- why the ideas about appropriate levels of punishment change
- how and why crime, punishment and policing have changed since 1450, and what similarities and differences there are over time
- what experiences men, women and children have had of the law since 1450 and why these experiences differ over time – and even during the same periods of time
- what role individuals play in causing change to happen and how their impact links with wider changes going on in their society
- what the key turning points are in changing experiences of crime, punishment and policing.

FASCINATING FACT

The past and the present can have some surprising similarities, as well as differences. For example, murder rates for East Anglia in the 14th century were similar to those of modern New York (USA)!

COPYRIGHT THIEVES!

JUST DOWNLOADING MUSIC!

Timeline

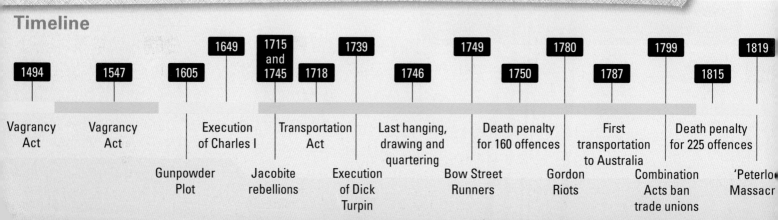

1494	Vagrancy Act
1547	Vagrancy Act
1605	Gunpowder Plot
1649	Execution of Charles I
1715 and 1745	Jacobite rebellions
1718	Transportation Act
1739	Execution of Dick Turpin
1746	Last hanging, drawing and quartering
1749	Bow Street Runners
1750	Death penalty for 160 offences
1780	Gordon Riots
1787	First transportation to Australia
1799	Combination Acts ban trade unions
1815	Death penalty for 225 offences
1819	'Peterloo Massacre

Hanging, drawing and quartering

A modern reconstruction of William Wallace (who resisted English efforts to conquer Scotland) being dragged to his execution in 1305. From the Middle Ages, until 1814, treason was punishable by hanging, drawing and quartering a living prisoner until they died. Why did rulers sometimes feel so under threat that they created such horrific punishments? And why, today, do we not execute any criminals?

18th-century smugglers

18th-century smugglers were 'criminals' (avoiding paying new taxes) to the government but 'local heroes' to many people because they made cheap goods easier to get hold of. We will be exploring how changes in society sometimes create new crimes, or stimulate old ones. And why different groups in society do not always agree on what is a 'crime'.

Modern riot

The Bradford riots in 2001, in West Yorkshire. These occurred as a result of tension between the city's ethnic and white communities. Violence on the streets is nothing new. In 1780 the Gordon Riots in London left 800 dead. One of the things we will be exploring is why violence such as this sometimes bursts onto the streets.

Activities

1 Look at the arguing heads. They disagree about the seriousness of crimes and how they should be dealt with. Why do people disagree in these ways?

What does this tell you about attitudes towards crime and punishment?

2 Look at the 'Fascinating fact'. Does this surprise you? Explain your answer.

A handful of examples of ways in which people disagree about how serious crimes are.

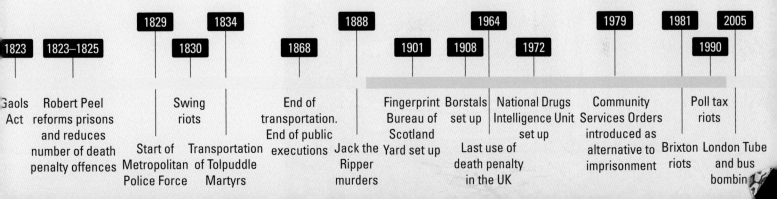

| 1823 | 1823–1825 | 1829 | 1830 | 1834 | 1868 | 1888 | 1901 | 1908 | 1964 | 1972 | 1979 | 1981 | 1990 | 2005 |

Gaols Act

Robert Peel reforms prisons and reduces number of death penalty offences

Start of Metropolitan Police Force

Swing riots

Transportation of Tolpuddle Martyrs

End of transportation. End of public executions

Jack the Ripper murders

Fingerprint Bureau of Scotland Yard set up

Borstals set up

Last use of death penalty in the UK

National Drugs Intelligence Unit set up

Community Services Orders introduced as alternative to imprisonment

Brixton riots

Poll tax riots

London Tube and bus bombing

1.1 Medieval ideas about different types of crime and punishments

4

Source A: Medieval hanging. Many medieval crimes were punishable by the death penalty of hanging. The death penalty is also known as capital punishment.

Medieval ideas about crime

Our study of crime and punishment starts in about AD1450. This is towards the end of the Middle Ages or the medieval period of history. Medieval crimes were divided according to how serious they were thought to be. There are some surprises. Stealing was put in the same group of serious crimes as murder and rape. This was because medieval society was set up with different groups of people having a place in it above, or below, other groups. Those with the most money and property wanted to protect it from those who had less, so they hanged thieves who threatened those who owned more.

There were also courts dealing with different groups of people. Royal Courts dealt with any serious crimes and all types of people. Church Courts dealt with priests, monks and nuns, and those breaking Church rules such as refusing to pay a tenth of their income to the Church. Manor Courts dealt with ordinary villagers in the countryside and made them keep to the rules set up by the local landowners (the lord of the manor).

Ways in which crimes judged in Royal Courts were divided according to their seriousness

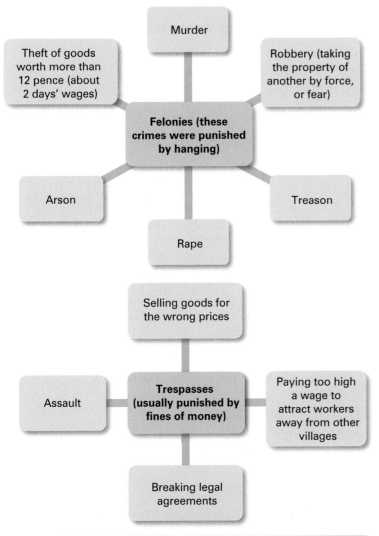

most likely to be fined and punished were unfree farmers called villeins. They could be fined for breaking a large number of rules that controlled their lives, but they had rights too and the Manor Court protected them from being made to do too much work or being fined too much.

Where are the prisons?

Prison, as a form of punishment, is largely a modern invention dating from the later 18th and early 19th centuries. It was not until 1576 that local judges were required to build 'houses of correction' in which beggars could be kept. Medieval prisons were mostly just for holding people waiting trial. Then, those found guilty were either hanged, fined, or forced to leave the country (outlawed). Because medieval judges believed they had been given power by God to kill or set free, they were ready to use hanging in many cases of crime. Anyone over the age of ten could be executed.

Activities

3 In what ways was the medieval system of imprisonment different from today?

The limits of justice

Only free men could appear in the Royal Courts. Women could only go to court to accuse someone who had: (a) murdered her husband (but only if he died in her arms), (b) attacked her and this led to the loss of an unborn child or (c) raped her.

Activities

1 Look at the picture of a medieval execution in Source A, opposite and the spider diagrams, above of crimes dealt with by Royal Courts. Why was the death penalty used for medieval crimes such as theft?

2 Explain how the way in which medieval society was divided up affected the kinds of courts and punishments different people faced.

In the Manor Courts

All kinds of aspects of life and minor crimes were controlled by the Manor Courts. The people

Summary

- Medieval crimes were divided into those considered more, or less, serious.
- Different courts existed for different groups of people.
- Different groups of people had different rights under the law.
- Prison was rarely used. Execution was common, as were fines.

1.2 Medieval ideas about preventing crime and catching criminals

Learning outcomes

By the end of this topic you should be able to:

● give some different reasons why crimes occur and how these can affect the 'crime-rate'

● explain the difference between 'crime prevention' and 'crime detection'

● identify ways in which medieval society was organised to try to prevent crime and to catch criminals

● explain why it was difficult to detect and prove medieval crime.

Factors affecting rates of crime

At different times changing events make it more likely that the amount of crime taking place will increase, or decrease. The 'amount of crime' taking place is called the 'crime-rate'.

Factors affecting the medieval 'crime-rate'.

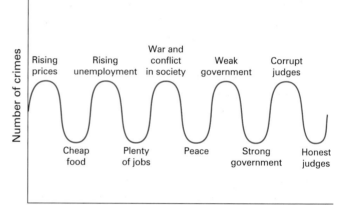

Events causing crime to go up or down

'Crime prevention' and 'crime detection'

Today, we have crime prevention such as:

● Neighbourhood Watch schemes

● burglar alarms
● CCTV
● police and community support officers on patrol
● the threat of fines and imprisonment.

Medieval authorities relied on:

● making groups of people responsible for each other's actions
● deterring people by the threat of punishment
● Church teachings about right and wrong.

When it comes to detecting criminals today we have:

● a police force
● the use of fingerprints
● DNA and other scientific evidence.

Source A: A medieval court, with a jury deciding guilt (or innocence) based on claims of witnesses and a person's past behaviour.

Medieval authorities relied on:

- catching a person as they committed a crime
- local people deciding if a neighbour was the kind of person likely to have committed a crime, based on past behaviour.

Activities

1 In small groups, create a 'spidergram' of reasons why people might commit crimes today. Beside each reason make a note of the kind of crime(s) this might lead to.

2 Write definitions of 'crime prevention' and 'crime detection'. What do these terms mean? For crime prevention and detection, write down some things that are available today, but that medieval authorities could not use. What did they use instead?

Medieval crimewaves

Evidence from the 14th and 15th centuries shows that more people were punished for stealing when unemployment increased. War caused increased crime too. Taxes went up to pay for armies and forced some people into poverty. This made them more likely to steal. Fighting between rival members of the royal family in the 15th-century 'Wars of the Roses' weakened local government and gave opportunities for criminals to commit crimes and escape punishment.

Medieval crime prevention

Medieval governments tried to prevent crimes from happening in a number of ways. For example, in 1285 it was ordered that a verge should be cleared of bushes for 200 feet (60 metres) on either side of a main road, to avoid providing cover for thieves.

All freemen (except for clergy and knights) were made to join a tithing of ten men, who were responsible for the behaviour of each other. If one of them was accused of a crime, the other members of the tithing had the job of bringing that person to justice, or paying a fine to the victim of the crime. If a crime was committed, they had to hunt for the criminal. This hunt was called the 'hue and cry'.

Medieval detectives?

When a person was brought to court, two methods were used to decide their guilt or innocence.

Witness of neighbours

The accused person would be judged innocent if he or she found enough people willing to swear on oath concerning their past good behaviour.

Trial by jury

This was the usual method by 1450. A group of local people looked at any evidence, listened to witnesses, discussed the character of the person accused of a crime – and made a decision.

Local crime catchers

With no police force, from the 12th century law enforcement relied on groups of local people bringing suspected criminals before a judge. By 1400 local landowners were appointed as Justices of the Peace to hold local courts at least four times a year to deal with less serious offences.

Activities

3 Choose and explain two reasons why medieval crime rates increased at certain times.

4 In pairs, decide the strengths and weaknesses of the two main medieval ways used to decide an accused person's guilt.

After…

By the end of the Middle Ages problems in the economy of the country were leading to an increase in unemployed people begging and looking for work. These beggars were increasingly treated as criminals.

Summary

- Medieval crime rates were affected by a range of causes.
- Medieval crime prevention relied on local communities.
- Without a police force and scientific methods, medieval crime detection was very difficult.

1.3 Punishing the poor: victims of poverty, or criminal beggars?

Learning outcomes

By the end of this topic you should be able to:

- understand ways in which social and economic changes can affect what is considered to be a crime
- explain why begging concerned wealthy and powerful people by the 16th century.

Treating beggars as criminals

Some actions are treated as crimes across the whole of the period from 1450 to today. Examples include murder and theft, but there are times in which particular problems lead to actions being punished, which would not be treated this way in a different period of time. In Elizabethan England in the 16th century, for example, there was great concern about the growing numbers of beggars. This led to these beggars being thought of as criminals – and punished.

Before...

Changes in the economy in the late 14th century and in the 15th century had increased the numbers of people wandering and looking for work. At the same time local people in juries and local judges called Justices of the Peace had been given more powers to keep law and order.

Activities

1 In pairs, discuss how (a) an unemployed cloth worker and (b) an Elizabethan landowner might feel about the growing number of beggars and the extent of the threat you feel they are to law and order.

Problems in the cloth industry increased the numbers of unemployed people.

Inflation caused prices to go up faster than wages.

Landowners kept sheep, instead of growing crops. This needed fewer workers.

Closure of monasteries took away support for the poor.

End of wars in England led to soldiers being out of work.

Population increase put pressure on jobs and food.

There was no national system to help the unemployed and sick.

Reasons why the number of beggars increased during the 16th century.

Large numbers of beggars travelling on the roads seemed to threaten a society where people were expected to know their place within their local community.

The cost of supporting beggars was resented by the communities they ended up in.

Acts of charity did not seem to be enough to meet the rising demand from the poor people.

Poor people were more likely to turn to other crimes such as theft.

Reasons why begging was treated harshly and as a crime.

Source A: A beggar is tied and whipped through the streets (1567).

Source B: Vagabonds and Beggars Act (1494).

'Vagabonds, idle and suspected persons shall be set in the stocks for three days and three nights and have none other sustenance but bread and water and then shall be put out of Town. Every beggar suitable to work shall resort to the Hundred where he last dwelled, is best known, or was born and there remain.'

Some places, such as York, issued badges to sick or injured beggars, who were thought to deserve help (the 'deserving poor'). This separated them from those considered lazy – called 'sturdy beggars'. In 1531 in a law passed by parliament, all beggars were to be classed as either deserving a licence and badge, or punished. Justices of the Peace put the new law into effect.

Wealthy people in parliament were so worried by begging that in 1547 the Vagrancy Act forced beggars to work. It also ordered that they should be whipped and branded. This law, though, was impossible to enforce and was repealed, but it shows how worried people were.

 Results**Plus**
Build better answers

What can you learn from Sources A and B about changes in how seriously begging was treated by the law? (4 marks)

◼ **Basic (1–2 marks)**
These answers give details from the sources but do not identify a change.

● **Good (3–4 marks)**
Good answers will identify a change and use information from both sources to support the statement about change.

Activities

2 What was the difference between a 'sturdy beggar' and one of the 'deserving poor'? How did the law treat them differently?

Summary

- Changes in society led to increased numbers of beggars and a 'moral panic'.
- This led to the treatment of healthy beggars as criminals.
- Despite the laws against begging, it was impossible to stop because it was brought on by wider social causes.

Who was driving these changes in the law?

Changes in the law and decisions about what should be regarded as criminal activity are sometimes led from the top (from government) and sometimes from below (from local communities putting pressure on government, or trying out ideas to combat crime).

1.4 Treason and plot! Why rulers felt under threat and the impact of this on the treatment of crime

Learning outcomes

By the end of this topic you should be able to:

- describe what the crime of treason involves
- explain why rulers in the 16th and 17th centuries felt particularly under threat.

Before...

Before 1485 charges of treason were used against those who rebelled against the king, but it was not until the reign of the Tudors that its use became frequent. This was because the Tudors had seized power at the end of a very unsettled time in English political history, known as the Wars of the Roses.

Rulers under threat

Treason is not a common crime, but the Tudors – who came to power in 1485 – were particularly concerned about it. This was because they had seized power by force and there were people who questioned their right to rule. Tensions increased when Henry VIII broke away from the Catholic Church. These religious tensions continued through the rules of Henry's son and daughters.

Then, on 5 November 1605, Catholic opponents attempted to murder King James I in the Guy Fawkes 'Gunpowder Plot'. The conspiritors planned to blow up the king, his family and leading Protestant aristocrats at the state opening of Parliament. After this, the plan was to start a rebellion and put a Catholic on the throne. There were a dozen leading conspirators, mostly from important Catholic families. Guy Fawkes was the explosives expert, responsible for igniting the large store of gunpowder the plotters had concealed in a cellar beneath the House of Lords. But the conspirators were betrayed. The leaders were

Source A: The executions of Guy Fawkes and the other plotters who attempted to blow up the king and parliament in 1605.

Activities

1   What can you learn from Source A about the attitude of the authorities to the crime of treason?

sentenced to be hanged, drawn and quartered. You can see what happened to them in Source A above.

In the 18th century, another change of royal family (from the Stuarts to the Hanoverians) led to yet more rebellions and charges of treason. Famous examples are the failed Scots rebellions of 1715 and 1745.

Executing traitors

Below are the words of the sentence of 'hanging, drawing and quartering'. These words were used until 1870 for those convicted of treason and sentenced to this terrible death.

After 1814, the convict would be hanged until dead and the mutilation would be carried out on their dead body.

> 'That you be drawn on a hurdle to the place of execution where you shall be hanged by the neck and being alive cut down, your privy members shall be cut off and your bowels taken out and burned before you, your head severed from your body and your body divided into four quarters to be disposed of at the King's pleasure.'

A short history of mutilation for treason

No one is sure exactly when the sentence of hanging, drawing and quartering was first used. The best evidence suggests that it began in the 13th century under King Edward I. He was attempting to impose English control on Wales and Scotland. His argument was that he was the rightful ruler of these countries and that anyone who opposed him was not a 'freedom fighter'

ResultsPlus
Top tip!

The punishment for treason at this time was so severe because the rulers were threatened by it. You will see how this is a common theme throughout the centuries – if rulers/governments fear something, then that becomes a crime and the punishment given depends on how serious the rulers think it is. The best candidates bring out these links in the exam and make connections between different time-periods.

but a 'traitor'. As a result, Edward used very brutal methods to make his point to those he considered 'traitors'. Hanging, drawing and quartering was one of the most obvious ways.

From this time onwards, it was the official punishment for anyone who tried to overthrow the king or queen. It was deliberately designed to show how terrible a crime this was thought to be. Since it was believed that God had given power to the king, treason was thought of as a crime against God as well as the king. The full sentence was usually reserved for commoners. Noble traitors were usually beheaded.

After...

By the late 18th century the charge of treason became rare. Amazingly, though, the official punishment for treason remained death until 1998. The last person to be executed for treason was William Joyce in 1946 for working for Nazi Germany during the Second World War.

Summary

- Political changes between 1485 and 1750 caused rulers to feel under threat.
- This led to an increase in accusations of treason.
- Earlier harsh punishments – designed to crush opposition to royal power – were increasingly used in this period of time.
- Lessening of political tension after 1750 reduced the use of such punishments.

Activities

2 Why did Edward I introduce a punishment as savage as hanging, drawing and quartering?

3 Why did the use of severe punishments for treason increase after 1485?

4 What does this tell you about the link between political events and the use of the law?

Challenge

5 Henry VIII frightened judges and juries so much that they delivered the verdict he wanted. This is legal, but some people think it is 'judicial murder' (legal but not right). What do you think? You might want to research more about those executed by Henry before making your decision.

1.5 Rulers and ruled: what beliefs affected attitudes towards crime and punishment, and who challenged the system?

Learning outcomes

By the end of this topic you should be able to:

- describe changing challenges to law and order
- explain how attitudes and beliefs in society affected definitions of 'crime'
- understand how authorities responded to challenges to the law
- describe how different groups of people had different experiences of both crime and punishment.

Before...

After a relatively stable period of time in the second half of the 15th century, population increase in the early 16th century coincided with growing demands for religious change and the start of Tudor rule, which caused many important social and religious changes at a time when rulers were feeling insecure.

Activities

1 Look at the causes of crime opposite, then look at the types of crime. Decide what would be the most likely cause of each type of crime and explain the connection between the two.

2 Which do you think was the most important of the causes of crime? Explain why you think this.

Causes of different types of crime

Causes of crime	Types of crime
Growth of towns	Refusal to follow official religious beliefs
Enclosure of land, including common land once used by all	Highwaymen on open roads, robbing travellers
Changes in religious beliefs	Beggars wandering from town to town
Increased unemployment	Footpads in dark alleys
Improved quality of roads	Hedge levelling to give access to common land again

Attitudes and beliefs

Divine right

It was believed that God gave power to kings and queens. People breaking the law were therefore challenging God and his representatives.

Hierarchy

There was a strong belief that society had a strict ordering with some groups of people above, or below, others in terms of power, wealth and rights. There was a sexual and age hierarchy too. Men were in charge of women. Adults had strict authority over children.

Property

The richest people owned the most property. Only wealthy people were represented in parliament, where laws were made. As a result, these laws protected the rights and property of the wealthy. Because of the belief in the divine right and hierarchy, rulers believed this was approved by God and that anyone who challenged this should be strongly punished. As a result, corporal punishment and capital punishment were commonly used.

Challenging the system

Increasing population

In 1450 the population of England was 2 million. By 1551 it had risen to 3 million and by 1750 it had more than doubled, to 7 million.

Increased urban growth and unemployment

In growing towns people were more difficult to control. The old world, where rulers knew the people they governed, was harder to maintain. This situation was made more difficult as unemployed people left their local areas to look for work.

Crimes against property

Most crimes committed by the poor were crimes against property, not crimes against the person. Street criminals were known as footpads. Due to better roads, road travel improved from 1700 to 1750 and the numbers of highwaymen increased. Dick Turpin – hanged in York in 1739 – was one of the most famous highwayman.

Changes in the countryside led to other types of crime. The setting out of country parks around great houses in the 17th century led to increased concerns about poaching. This was a 'social crime' (an activity that was made illegal, although in different circumstances it would have been allowed).

Ordinary people had for centuries believed that custom gave them the right to hunt animals like rabbits and hares for food in the woods and heaths around their villages. However, landowners increasingly restricted this sort of use of their property and began to use the law to punish those caught poaching. Poachers, in turn, sometimes organised themselves into gangs so they could fight off anyone trying to arrest them.

Early smugglers

Another social crime is smuggling. In 1614 exporting wool was made illegal and in 1661 it was made punishable by death. The effect of the first law was to encourage smugglers to take wool out of the country illegally. The second law made it more likely that they would carry weapons to resist arrest. Increased taxes on tea and brandy made it profitable by the 1730s for smugglers to bring these items into the country. The profits to be made from this illegal trade led to the formation of well-organised gangs. Between 1735 and 1749 the Hawkhurst Gang dominated smuggling from Kent to Dorset.

Activities

Challenge

5 'Government action can sometimes lead to increases, instead of decreases, in crime.' How far was this true in the case of smuggling between 1614 and 1750?

Activities

3 Explain how divine right, a hierarchical society and belief in the importance of property impacted on attitudes towards crime and punishment.

4 Decide what you think were the three main challenges to the way society was run in the period up to 1750. For each one explain (a) why it was a challenge and (b) the kinds of crimes that this challenge led to.

Summary

- Laws protected the rights and property of the wealthy.
- Most crimes committed by the poor were crimes against property.
- As population rose and more people lived in towns, rulers found it hard to control the population.
- Social crimes, like poaching and smuggling, became a greater challenge to authority.

1.6 Rulers and ruled: how did rulers meet the challenges they faced?

Learning outcomes

By the end of this topic you should be able to:

- identify methods used to deter crime
- explain the difference between deterrence and retribution.

Punishments to deter crime in different ways

Source A: Punishment in the stocks (17th century).

Source B: Crowds at a public hanging (mid-18th century).

Source C: In 1656 James Naylor was whipped, a hot iron bored though his tongue and his face branded with a 'B' for Blasphemy for claiming that he was Jesus Christ.

Activities

1 Describe each of the punishments being used in Sources A–C.
2 Explain, for each, why magistrates and judges might have thought it was a useful form of punishment.

Criminalising beggars

Begging was regarded as a crime. Other wanderers were even more harshly punished. In 1554 a law was passed that allowed gypsies to be hanged.

Different experiences of the law

Punishments varied according to a person's social group. Commoners were hanged, drawn and quartered for treason but nobles were beheaded. Until the 18th century, any first-time offender who claimed benefit of clergy (they were able to read a passage from the Bible) was often acquitted. Originally, this had been done so that a member of the clergy (e.g. a priest) could prove that they should be tried in a Church Court. Women and men were also treated differently. Women who murdered their husband were burnt at the stake because a husband was thought to be the natural master of his wife. By the 18th century, the woman was often strangled before being burnt.

The use of fear

Lacking a real prison system, the punishment of criminals depended on either (a) removing them from society (by execution), (b) fining them, or (c) hurting or humiliating them. This was often done by putting someone in the stocks, or pillory. The aim was a mixture of retribution (punishment) and deterrence (preventing crime).

The 'Bloody Code' and the start of transportation

Source D: The number of crimes carrying the death penalty.

Year	Number of crimes carrying death penalty
1688	50
1765	160
1815	225

Later historians used the phrase the 'Bloody Code' to describe the number of crimes carrying the death penalty from the late 17th to the early 19th centuries (including stealing sheep, damaging trees and stealing rabbits). These severe punishments were intended to deter people from committing crimes. In fact, the 'Bloody Code' failed in its aim. Many juries refused to find a person guilty if a death penalty would follow. Fewer people were hanged in the 18th century under the 'Bloody Code' than in the previous century. As a result, in 1823, Sir Robert Peel reduced the number of crimes punishable by capital punishment by over 100 offences.

From the 17th century until American Independence in 1776, convicts were also transported to the Caribbean and to North America to be used as labourers on plantations. They could

also be transported for political crimes. (For more on transportation, see topic 2.5 on page 26.)

Modern people are usually very critical of 18th-century punishments. This is because 21st-century values and attitudes towards crime and punishment are very different from those of the 18th century. This reminds us that, while some ideas about crime remain fairly constant, others vary according to the values of society.

Activities

3 Explain the difference between 'retribution' and 'deterrence'.

4 Explain, with examples, how the law in the 18th century was applied differently to different groups in society. Does this suggest 'change' or 'continuity' from the medieval period?

5 How successful was the 'Bloody Code'? Explain: (a) its aims, (b) its effect on the law and punishments, and (c) your conclusion on whether it met its aims.

Activities

Challenge

6 Why is it that many people today are shocked by 18th-century punishments?

Summary

- Attempting to protect property and keep people in 'their places' led to the harsh treatment of those who threatened these areas of life.
- The period up to 1750 saw increasing changes to traditional society, which led to new crimes and treatment of these crimes.
- A range of public punishments were used to tackle crime, which became more severe during the 18th century.
- The 'Bloody Code' was less effective in meeting its aims than its supporters intended.

1.7 The work of the historian: the career of Jonathan Wild

Jonathan Wild (1683–1725) was the most famous criminal in 18th-century Britain. He ran a successful gang of thieves and at the same time seemed to be the most successful policeman in the country. Wild kept the goods his gang stole. He waited for the newspapers to report the crime, then he would claim that his 'agents' had recovered the stolen items. He would return these goods for a reward. As well as pretending to find stolen goods, he also 'caught' thieves. These were really rivals, or members of his own gang who had refused to obey him. In 1718, Wild gave himself the title 'Thief Taker General of Great Britain and Ireland'. He claimed to have had over sixty thieves hanged. He became a popular figure in the newspapers. This popularity collapsed when his criminal activities were finally exposed. He was hanged at Tyburn, London, in 1725.

Source A: Jonathan Wild was pelted with stones on the way to his execution (drawn in the mid-18th century).

Source B: An 'invitation' to the execution of Jonathan Wild, produced by one of Wild's opponents (from the time of Wild's death in 1725).

Source D: From *The Life of Jonathan Wild, From His Birth to His Death*, by 'H.D', Clerk to 'Justice R.', 1725. The writer disguised his name but suggested he had good information since he worked for a judge (whose name he partly hides – but readers at the time would easily have been able to identify the judge).

'When things are rightly compared, it will be found that [Wild] had a more difficult game to play; for he blinded the eyes of the world, found out tricks to evade the penalties of the law; and on the other side, governed a body of people who were enemies to all government; and made them obey.'

Watch out!

Many students waste precious exam time by only describing what is in the sources. You will not get any marks for doing this, so remember to get straight on with answering the question and only refer to information that supports your answer.

Source C: From the novel *Jonathan Wild*, written by Henry Fielding in 1743. Although based on the life of Wild, Fielding turned it into a novel in which he criticised the state of London in the early 18th century and the kinds of people who were thought to be 'great' and 'heroic' by the public and newspapers.

'One instance shows our hero's character even to his last moment… Wild, in the midst of the shower of stones etc., which played upon him, applied his hand to the parson's pocket, and emptied it of his bottle screw [corkscrew], which he carried out of the world in his hand.'

Activities

These questions are exam-style questions for those students studying Unit 3D, The work of the historian.

1 Study Sources A and B.

   What can you learn from Sources A and B about how Jonathan Wild's execution was regarded at the time?

2 Study Sources C and D.

   How much of Fielding's account in Source C do you think is reliable?

   Explain your answer, using Sources C and D.

3 Study Sources C and D.

   Which of Sources C and D would be more useful to a historian trying to explain why Wild made such an impact on the opinions of people living in the 1720s?

   Explain your answer, using Sources C and D.

2.1 The impact of industrial and agricultural change on crime and punishment

Learning outcomes

By the end of this topic you should be able to:

- identify major changes affecting society after 1750
- explain the impact of these changes on crimes against the person, property and authority
- evaluate the ways in which responses of those in authority met these challenges.

Before...

Before 1750 society was already changing. The growth in population had led to an increase in crime in cities such as London. This had also given opportunities to criminals, such as Jonathan Wild (see pages 16–17), in the absence of an effective police force.

Changes affecting society after 1750

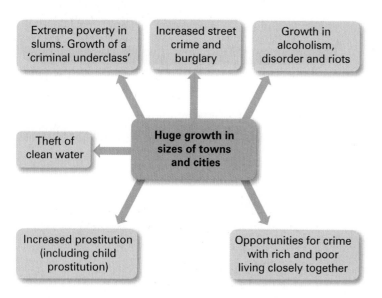

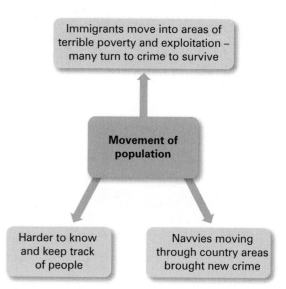

Activities

1 From the spider diagrams above, look at the changes brought about by the Industrial Revolution after 1750. In your own words, explain how each change had an impact on the experiences of crime.

2 Which of the two main areas of change do you think would have been the biggest cause of increased crime? Explain why.

Crime in industrial cities

Gustav Doré worked in London for three months every year, for five years, producing drawings that eventually appeared in a book entitled *London: A Pilgrimage*, which was published in 1872. It gives a shocking view of the situation in the poorest areas. See Source A for an example of Dore's drawings.

Source A: Wentworth Street, in the slum area of Whitechapel. Drawn by Gustav Doré and published in *London: A Pilgrimage*, 1872.

Activities

3 Imagine you are visiting Whitechapel (Source A). Write a report describing the area, criminal dangers and how safe you feel. Read your report to a neighbour and compare your 'experience'.

Source B: Map showing the number of criminal offenders to every 10,000 of population in each county of England and Wales. Figures taken from *London Labour and the London Poor*, by Henry Mayhew, published in 1861.

The orange areas show increased crime – these are areas of growing population (e.g. London and the West Midlands) as well as a few country areas.

Northumberland 8.2
Cumberland 7.1
Durham 7.8
Westmorland 8.1
Yorkshire 11.4
Lancaster 18.5
Chester 22.6
Derby 10.5
Nottingham 11.8
Lincoln 12.8
North Wales 7.2
Shropshire 14.9
Stafford 17.9
Leicester 17.1
Rutland 13.9
Norfolk 17.1
Warwick 25.6
Northampton 14.2
Huntingdon 14.1
Cambridge 14.7
Suffolk 15.7
Worcester 25.0
Hereford 23.8
Bedford 15.2
South Wales 8.4
Oxford 17.8
Buckingham 20.4
Hertford 17.5
Essex 19.1
Gloucester 26.1
Monmouth 18.0
Middlesex 24.5
Berks 12.9
Wilts 18.9
Surrey 16.3
Kent 16.4
Somerset 19.9
Hants 17.7
Sussex 15.3
Devon 14.1
Dorset 14.3
Cornwall 8.0

Activities

4 Why would Whitechapel have been a difficult area to police, even after the creation of the Metropolitan Police Force in 1829?

5 As a class, discuss Source B. How can you explain the distribution of the areas of crime? Are there any surprises in this distribution?

Can we trust the evidence of Doré?

Not everyone thought Doré presented a balanced view of life in industrial London. Some critics complained that he only focused on poverty. Doré was accused by the *Art Journal* of 'inventing rather than copying.'

Activities

Challenge

6 Why did some people criticise Doré? Why might this affect how we use his work as evidence for life in London? What evidence would you need to examine, in order to assess how useful his work really is for a historian studying poverty and the criminal underclass?

After…

Faced with the difficulty of keeping order and tackling crime in early 19th-century London, the Home Secretary, Sir Robert Peel, set up the Metropolitan Police Force in 1829. Soon the idea was copied across the country.

Summary

- Massive economic and social changes took place after 1750. This led to an increase in crime and disorder.
- Many of these crimes were crimes against property and were committed by poor people struggling to survive.
- The violent state of the worst slums meant that crimes against people increased too.

2.2 The impact of industrial and agricultural change: how governments responded to threats to authority

20

Learning outcomes

By the end of this topic you should be able to:

● explain why violent unrest was such a challenge to government

● describe the strategies that governments used to meet these challenges.

Before...

In the period 1800–15 more soldiers were protecting factories against *Luddites* (workers breaking machines that took their jobs) in northern England than were fighting the French in the Napoleonic War. Without a police force it was hard to control this unrest.

Source A: A cartoon depicting the 'Peterloo Massacre', 1819. It was named 'Peterloo' as a sarcastic reference to the famous British victory over the French at Waterloo in 1815. It was drawn shortly after the event by George Cruikshank and based on accounts of what happened. The artist himself

Massacre at St Peters or "BRITONS STRIKE HOME"!!!

Source B: *The Peterloo Massacre*, 1819. It was painted in 1980 and based on accounts of the event.

Challenges to authority

● Poor living and working conditions made many workers desperate for reforms.

● The Revolution in France in 1789 encouraged some people to hope for a similar change in the system in Britain.

● Many people made more moderate demands: the right to vote, the right to strike, the right to criticise the government.

● The government had no police force until 1829, so it used soldiers to put down uprisings and revolutionary meetings.

● The government also used laws to control people who protested at how Britain was being run.

Activities

1 How did the government respond to those who challenged its authority?

2 Look at Sources A and B. What do they show about the reaction of the authorities to protests?

How did governments deal with unrest?

After the outbreak of revolution in France in 1789, the British government and upper classes felt very vulnerable. In order to prevent such a revolution happening in Britain, they attempted to repress any people and groups who seemed to be challenging the way Britain was ruled. They used: (a) new laws and (b) force to keep control.

In 1817 *habeas corpus* was suspended, which meant that prisoners could be held without trial. In 1819 groups demanding the reform of parliament and the right to vote met at St Peter's Fields, Manchester. Attempting to force their way through the crowd of 50,000 people to arrest leading speakers, soldiers called yeomanry (who witnesses claimed had been drinking) drew their swords. A total of 18 unarmed civilians were killed and 500 were injured. It became known as the 'Peterloo Massacre'. Following this, the Six Acts of Parliament were passed that banned civilians training with weapons, reduced rights to bail, banned unauthorised meetings, increased sentences for criticising the government and made it expensive to publish cheap newspapers.

The Tolpuddle Martyrs – using the law to control threats to the wealthy

In 1833, a peaceful group of Dorset farm workers from the village of Tolpuddle formed a trade union to try to stop their wages going down. They were not acting violently but the local rich farmers feared they might lose control of their workers. The government shared their fears. Like the farmers, they were worried that the farm workers in Tolpuddle were challenging their right to control the country to suit the richest members of society.

How was the government going to react? What could it do? This time, it did not use violence because the Tolpuddle farm workers were not violent and could not be described as revolutionaries. Instead, the law was used to control them. A law from 1797 that existed to stop the swearing of secret oaths in the navy was used to arrest them. It had been designed to stop mutinies but it could be used against the farm workers because they had sworn a secret oath not to tell anyone about their meetings. This fact was now used against them. The farm workers were arrested and transported to Australia for seven years. After huge protests the 'Tolpuddle Martyrs' were eventually released in 1836.

Activities

3 Explain how the government sometimes made criminals out of people demanding reforms in the early 19th century.

Challenge

4 Which of Sources A and B would be more useful to a historian trying to find out what happened in this event?

After...

During the later years of the 19th century governments used reform to improve conditions. This reduced protests and was a better way to deal with unrest than with the army or harsh laws.

Summary

- Revolutionary ideas and economic problems led to the government feeling under threat.
- People demanding reform were treated as criminals.
- There were some violent challenges to authority.
- Reforms after 1850 meant that demands for change were no longer treated as crimes.

2.3 Smugglers: criminals or popular heroes?

22

Learning outcomes

By the end of this topic you should be able to:

- explain why smuggling and poaching were regarded as serious crimes
- explain why there were such different contemporary opinions about whether these actions were crimes.

Before...

Large-scale smuggling started in about 1300, when a customs duty was placed on the export of English wool.

Source A: *The Smugglers*, by George Morland, painted in 1792.

Source B: A smuggler and his family, painted in 1825.

WILL WATCH,
THE SMUGGLER BOLD.

Published Sep 24, 1825

Smuggling: a government-made problem?

Smuggling in the 18th and early 19th centuries is often seen as a problem made by the government. The decision to raise large amounts of money by taxing goods coming into the country created a situation where huge amounts of money could be made by bringing goods into the country illegally. Smuggling met the huge demand for these goods.

Activities

1 Look at the timeline. Choose two events that were important in causing the growth of smuggling. Explain why. Then explain why widespread smuggling came to an end.

Key changes in smuggling and actions designed to stop it.

1660	1690s	1690	1700	1740s	1745	1759	1792–1815	1850
Export of wool made illegal	Excise duty extended from chocolate, coffee, tea, beer, cider and spirits to cover salt, leather and soap	Mounted customs officers established	Waterguard established with ships to patrol coast	Growth of armed smuggling gangs	Tax on tea reduced. Smugglers turned to smuggling spirits	Cost of fighting wars led to increased tax on imports	Widespread smuggling of French goods (during war with France)	Taxes on imported goods cut. Period of large-scale smuggling over

Criminals or popular heroes?

Because the actual goods brought into the country were legal and harmless, many people were sympathetic towards smugglers. They thought it was the government that was acting unreasonably. Crimes such as smuggling, which do not actually harm anyone but are still illegal, are sometimes called 'social crimes'. The harsh punishments reserved for smugglers only added to this sympathy. Large numbers of people near the coasts were involved in active smuggling, hiding contraband, providing alibis for smugglers and trading with them. Many more – inland – bought the smuggled goods.

This created a situation where there was a huge difference between the official and the popular view of smuggling and its status as a crime. People regarded as criminals by the government became popular heroes. Their popularity hid the fact that many smugglers were prepared to use extreme violence in order to intimidate witnesses, kill informers or fight off customs officers.

Source C: Words on the grave of a smuggler killed in cross-fire with customs officers near Poole, Dorset, 1765.

'To the memory of Robert Trotman, who was barbarously murdered on the shore near Poole.'

Activities

2 In pairs, create two arguments: (a) that smugglers were criminals; (b) that they were popular heroes. Now present your arguments to each other. Give each other a score of 1–5 (1 = low, 5 = high) on how well you think the other person's argument was presented.

Today, some people have similar views on smuggling. While most would be shocked about the smuggling of drugs, guns, explosives or people, there are many who would take less seriously the smuggling of alcohol or cigarettes for personal use. This attitude is very similar to that held by smugglers' sympathisers in the late 18th and early 19th centuries. But these are all criminal offences, although the impact on individuals and on society does, of course, differ.

Activities

Challenge

3 'Smuggling is an example of a crime created by government policy.' To what extent do you agree with this view? Think of why smuggling occurs, attitudes to different types of smuggling, and whether the same answer can apply to all types of smuggling.

ResultsPlus
Build better answers

Why were the laws against smuggling so difficult to enforce in the 18th and early 19th centuries? Source C may help you with your answer. (12 marks)

■ **Basic (1–4 marks)**
These answers usually make general comments about smuggling, not about why it was hard to enforce.

● **Good (5–8 marks)**
Answers will describe aspects of smuggling such as how it was carried out or public support for smugglers, but will not explain why this made it hard to enforce the law.

▲ **Excellent (9–12 marks)**
Answers will explain factors making law enforcement difficult, such as the methods used by smugglers themselves, support from the population or the difficulty in patrolling all parts of the coast. Each reason will be supported by information.

After...

Reducing taxes on imported goods in the 1840s put an end to large-scale smuggling. In the 20th century profits from illegal drugs led to a new wave of smuggling.

Summary

- Tax increases on certain items encouraged smuggling.
- Smugglers created organised gangs and many people were involved.
- In response, the government reorganised coastal customs checks.

2.4 From prevention to detection: the creation of the modern police force

Learning outcomes

By the end of this topic you should be able to:

● describe the methods of preventing crime and catching criminals that existed before 1829 and explain the limitations of these methods

● explain why the Metropolitan Police Force was established in 1829

● understand changing public attitudes towards the police

● explain how the role and impact of policing changed over the 19th century.

Source A: A cartoon drawn in 1838 by George Cruikshank, included in Dickens's 'Mudfog Papers' published in Bentley's *Miscellany*. The work suggested that 'harmless and wholesome recreation for the young noblemen of England' would be to beat up model policemen. It suggests there was little affection or respect for the police.

Automaton Police Office, and real Offenders.

FROM THE MODEL EXHIBITED BEFORE SECTION B. OF THE MUD FOG ASSOCIATION.

The problems with existing police forces

When the magistrate Henry Fielding established the Bow Street Runners in 1749, this improved crime detection a little. However, they did not patrol so did not contribute to crime prevention. When, after 1754, his brother – John Fielding – established mounted patrols, this gave the force a presence on the streets. Nevertheless, the Bow Street policemen were not present in sufficient numbers to meet the needs of London. This meant that magistrates usually relied on criminals

Bow Street Horse Patrols. Operated out of Bow Street courts, London. Patrolled London streets. Only a small number.

Part-time soldiers of yeomanry and regular troops. Could be used to put down riots or rebellions.

Bow Street Runners. Founded in 1749 by Henry Fielding with his brother, John Fielding. Operated out of Bow Street courts, London. Tracked down criminals and stolen property. Only a small number.

Policing before 1829

Parish constables. Dealt with minor disorder and beggars; arrested petty criminals.

Watchmen or 'Charlies' (because they were set up under Charles II). Kept an eye on property in London. Usually old, poorly paid and organised by parish constables.

Activities

1 In small groups, look back at topics 2.1 and 2.2. Why did changes after 1750 mean that the police forces on the spider diagram above were unable to cope with the situation they faced?

2 What problems might be caused by relying on soldiers to control crowds? Look at topic 2.2 to help with this answer.

Source B: 'Familiar figures of London: the Policeman', produced in 1901. What does this picture and its title suggest about attitudes to police by the 1900s?

being caught in the act or being given away by informers. When there was large-scale disorder, it was necessary to bring in soldiers. This often led to deaths and this problem was seen when soldiers were used at 'Peterloo' in 1819 (see pages 20–21).

Towards a real police force: the work of Sir Robert Peel

In 1829, the Home Secretary, Sir Robert Peel, persuaded parliament to pass the Metropolitan Police Act. This established the first permanent, uniformed police force in London. Peel is an example of an individual who had a great effect on history. He believed that the best way for government to keep control was by carrying out policing in a way that did not add to tensions in society: he did not want the new police to look like the army. As a well-respected politician, he was able to persuade parliament that this was the best approach to deal with crime and keep order on the streets. He was helped by being able to point to successful earlier attempts to create small police forces.

While the new police did catch criminals, one of their main effects was to deter crime. Soon cities and counties around the country were copying

the example of London in setting up a police force. Reactions to the new police force were mixed. When PC Robert Culley was killed in 1833, a jury decided this was 'justifiable homicide' (not illegal). Soon, however, the police patrols became an important deterrent to crime, and uniformed policemen and detectives became skilled catchers of criminals. Still, until the use of fingerprints and other scientific aids in the 20th century many crimes were very difficult to solve.

Improved pay and training meant that the police developed a reputation for honesty. This increased public trust. Targeting uniformed patrols in high crime areas helped to reduce street crimes and disorder. In 1842, a detective department was set up in London to solve crimes, not just to prevent them. In 1878 this became known as the CID. In 1901, the first Fingerprint Bureau was set up in Scotland Yard, which increased the numbers of crime solved by the CID. This, along with the use of photographs of suspects, assisted crime detection with new technology.

Activities

3   Imagine you were Sir Robert Peel in 1829. Write a speech to parliament explaining the need for a new police force. In it: (a) explain the problems facing law and order, (b) give reasons why the existing police force cannot cope and (c) suggest your answer to this problem.

4   What can you learn from Sources A and B about changing attitudes towards the police in London between 1838 and 1901?

Challenge

5   Why might creating a better paid police force improve policing?

Summary

- From the 17th century, efforts had been made to improve policing in London. These efforts increased during the 18th century.
- After 1829, a well-organised police force could tackle both crime prevention and, eventually, detection.

2.5 Changes in punishment

Learning outcomes

By the end of this topic you should be able to:

- explain why attitudes towards crime and punishment meant that transportation was used from the 17th century onwards
- explain why the place of transportation shifted from North America to Australia in the late 18th century
- understand why transportation came to an end.

Before...

Crimes against property were severely punished. With no national prison system, this meant that criminals who damaged or stole from property were often executed. Searching for a more humane solution led to the start of transportation.

Why were criminals transported to Australia?

No national prison system to house large numbers of criminals. Where to send them?

Lost control of America after 1776. Where to send criminals now?

Tradition since 17th century of transporting criminals to colonies. Is this the answer to growing crime?

In 1770, Eastern Australia claimed for Britain. A possible place for convicts? They could provide workers.

Transportation to Australia

By 1780s, British prisons and hulks overcrowded and diseased. How to solve this?

Belief that crimes against property deserve heavy punishment to deter criminals. What will work?

Increasing petty crime in growing cities. What to do with petty criminals?

Despite the 'Bloody Code' many feel execution is too harsh for petty crime. What punishment to use?

Activities

1 Explain why transportation to Australia seemed to offer an answer to the problems of dealing with petty criminals in the late 18th century. Use Sources A and B in your answer.

How events can combine to cause change to happen

Transportation is a good example of how: (a) previous systems of punishment and definitions of crime, (b) changing ideas about the right levels of punishment and deterrence and (c) other factors can combine to cause events to happen and ways of doing things to develop.

Source A: Convicts doing hard labour under military guard on Norfolk Island, between Australia and New Zealand, 1847.

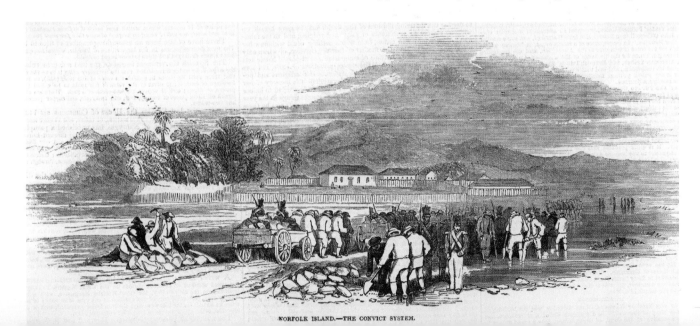

NORFOLK ISLAND.—THE CONVICT SYSTEM.

Since the Middle Ages crimes against property were more severely punished than they are today. Without a prison system, many petty criminals were hanged.

From the early 17th century some people in authority thought execution was too harsh a punishment for petty crime. But this came at the same time as an increase in petty crime in the late 17th and 18th centuries. Transporting criminals to work as labourers in the new British colonies, first in America and then in Australia seemed the answer. It was a harsh punishment to deter others, but was more humane than hanging and it provided free workers.

Source B: Examples of crimes leading to transportation. From Nottingham Borough Quarter Sessions Court.

ASHWORTH, Joseph
6 April 1841: Transported 10 yrs for stealing 4 pennies.
CLARKE, John
16 Oct 1828: Transported 7 yrs for stealing 2 coats.

The end of transportation

Transportation was abolished in 1868. In total, 160,023 people were transported to Australia. Transportation ended for a number of reasons: (a) Australia no longer had a need for forced labourers and did not want the kinds of people that transportation brought; (b) since the 1820s an improved prison system in Britain offered an alternative to transportation; (c) many people in Britain began to question the use of transportation. Some felt it was too expensive and was not a deterrent since it gave criminals the chance of a new life after their sentence. Others began to see it as too harsh a punishment, just as execution for theft had once been.

Activities

2 In your own words explain why transportation to Australia took place and why it ended.

3 Prepare a debate around the title 'The move to transportation should be thought of as *progress* in the punishment of crime'. One group argues *for* this point of view. One group argues *against*. Then describe what you think is the case and why.

The end of public execution

Public executions were banned in Britain in 1869, but there had been campaigns to end them for many decades. The Bloody Code had focused on the spectacle of execution: the idea that people watching such harsh punishment being carried out would be deterred from committing crimes themselves. But many commentators pointed out that few spectators seemed to be deterred at all. Pickpocketing was very common in the crowds watching an execution – even if the victim was themselves a pickpocket! The atmosphere at a hanging was often more like a carnival than a sombre lesson in the consequences of crime. And public executions often saw the crowd showing sympathy for the victim; sometimes there were even riots against the authorities. So although the last public execution was as late as 1869, the procession of the condemned to the London gallows at Tyburn ended in 1783, nearly a century before.

Activities

Challenge

4 Charles Dickens was hugely influential social commentator. He was a strong opponent of public executions and started arguing for their abolition in the 1840s. Why do you think it took another twenty years before they were banned?

After...

With the end of transportation and reductions in the use of the death penalty, imprisonment in the new prisons in Britain became the usual punishment for petty crime.

Summary

- Transportation was a more humane punishment than execution.
- By the 1860s changes in British prisons and attitudes in Australia led to the end of transportation.

2.6 How successful were 19th-century prison reformers?

Learning outcomes

By the end of this topic you should be able to:

- identify different reasons for the use of prisons and explain why imprisonment increased in the 18th and 19th centuries
- describe prison conditions and the work of reformers John Howard and Elizabeth Fry
- assess how successful the prisoner reformers were.

Before...

Prison was rarely used as a punishment for crime. Hanging, fining and corporal punishment were the usual punishments used but from the 18th century the use of prisons increased.

Retribution
To punish people for doing wrong.

Deterrence
To discourage others from committing crimes.

Removal
To keep them away from society to protect others.

Restitution
To work to make a payment back to society.

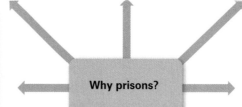
Why prisons?

Rehabilitation/reform
To change a person for the better.

Why were there calls for the reform of prisons?

John Howard was born in 1726. Appointed High Sheriff of Bedfordshire, he was appalled by conditions in the county gaol. Howard toured Britain and Europe in the 1770s and 1780s to try to discover better ways of running prisons. He called for prisoners to have Christian teaching, work and decent food, and visits by chaplains and doctors. He wanted prisons to be cleaned and prison guards to be paid. As a result of his work, parliament passed the 1774 Gaol Act, which suggested ways for improving health and sanitation. Although most gaolers ignored this, Howard's ideas were important because later reformers built on his work and took it forward.

The Quaker Elizabeth Fry was born in 1780 and, like Howard, was motivated by her Christian faith. In Newgate Prison, London, Fry found women and children living in conditions of violence and disease, and she was determined to show God's love to them and try to reform them. She set up education classes and treated the prisoners with kindness and respect; she suggested rules and the prisoners voted on them. In 1825 Fry published her ideas on how to improve prisons. This spread her ideas and helped to change attitudes.

The prison reformers were remarkable people, but the story of prison reform in the 19th century reveals how change is caused by the interaction of individuals and larger institutions, such as government. Howard and Fry could not have made a big difference by themselves.

The work of Sir Robert Peel

Fry's work coincided with Sir Robert Peel's time as Home Secretary. The slow growth in demands for change and the example of Fry's work persuaded Peel that action was needed. The Gaols Act (1823) paid gaolers. It also provided work for prisoners, women gaolers for women prisoners, inspections of prisons, visits by chaplains and doctors, and basic education. In the 1830s prisoners were given clean, separate cells and more work. A huge new prison-building programme took place. The first was at Pentonville, London, in 1842. By 1877 some 90 new prisons had been built. As well as reforming the prision system, Peel also reduced the number of death penalty offences.

Source A: *Separate Cell in Pentonville Prison*, 1862. With a bed and weaving loom in the cell, the prisoner would have had almost no contact with other prisoners.

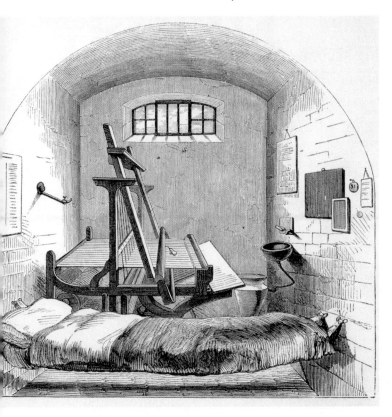

Source B: *Tread-Wheel and Oakum-Shed at the City Prison*, Holloway, 1862. Oakum picking is the unravelling and cleaning of rope. Both activities were done in silence, avoiding contact with others.

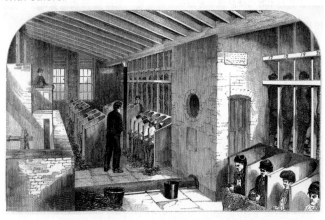

How successful were the reformers?

Progress was not exactly as Howard or Fry wanted. They wanted rehabilitation/reform. Many in government wanted retribution and deterrence. Reforms were made to stop prisoners learning criminal skills from one another. The **Separate System** (Source A) and the **Silent System** (Source B) were introduced in the mid-19th century. Although these systems aimed to reform prisoners, the lack of contact with others drove many of them to commit suicide.

After...

Today, some 19th century prisons are still used but house more people than they were designed for.

Summary

• The work of prison reformers led to improvements in prison conditions.

• Prisons in the 19th century were a compromise between rehabilitation and retribution.

2.7 The work of the historian: was violent crime increasing in Victorian London?

Many people in Victorian London feared violent crime. An example was in 1888, when the country was horrified by the brutal murder of women in the Whitechapel area of London. These were the 'Jack the Ripper' killings that resulted in the deaths of at least five women, beginning with Mary Ann Nichols, who was murdered on 31 August, and ending with Mary Jane Kelly, who was murdered on 9 November.

Earlier, in the 1850s there had been a panic over 'garrotters' – street criminals who strangled victims, with rope, to rob them.

But was London in the second half of the 19th century really becoming more violent? And if it wasn't, why did people at the time think that it was?

Source B: From *The Illustrated London News* 5 July 1873. Popular, cheap, illustrated newspapers returned to the fear of garrotters in the 1870s – twenty years after such newspapers had first carried similar reports.

'A gang of garrotters in Lambeth, led by a youth known as "The Black Prince" has devised a new method of relieving victims of diamond rings. One of them seized the jewelled finger and hammered it with a heavy instrument, which broke the bone; the finger was then twisted round till it came out of the socket. Here the operation was interrupted and the garrotters had to decamp with only a gold watch and chain.'

Source A: 'The Whitechapel Monster again seen seeking another victim', from *The Illustrated Police News*, published on 1 December 1888. From the mid 19th century, cheap newspapers carried lurid, illustrated accounts of murders.

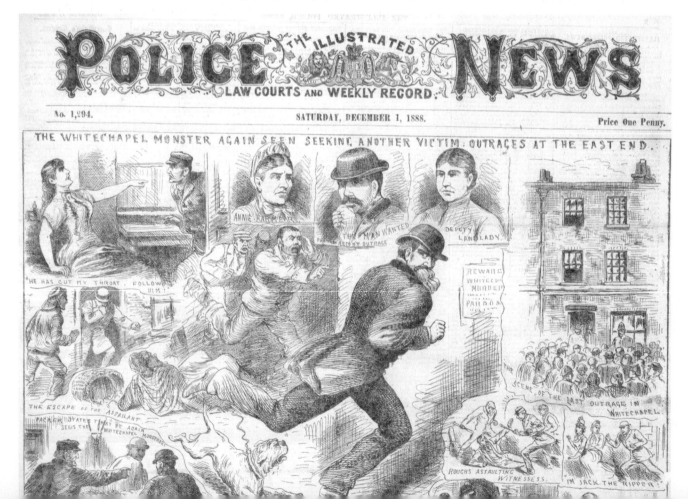

Source C: From the humorous newspaper, *Punch*, 14 March 1857. The caption reads: 'Elderly Gentleman thinks that Garrotting's come to a pretty pass when it's openly practised in broad daylight. Where *are* the Police?' He has really just been caught by accident in a girl's skipping rope.

Elderly Gentleman thinks that Garotting's come to a pretty pass when it's openly practised in broad daylight. Where are the Police?

Source D: From *Men of Blood*, by Martin J. Wiener, 2004.

'Officially recorded homicides fell in England from something like 20 per 100,000 annually in medieval times to about one per 100,000 at the opening of the 20th century… just when one might have expected a relaxation of the drive… to suppress violence, instead the Victorian era saw a major intensification. Crimes of violence came to be taken more seriously by the state than ever before. It may at first puzzle us that, while (as we know) the recorded homicide rate had fallen to its lowest level in English history, and lesser violence had probably also diminished, both officials and members of the writing and reading public exhibited greater fear and outrage in the face of interpersonal violence than ever before.'

Source E: From *Hard Men: The English and Violence Since 1750,* by Clive Emsley, 2005.

'The statistics reveal property crime to have been far more significant than violent crime in Victorian and Edwardian England. They also show a general decline in theft and violence from the mid 19th century to the First World War. There were occasional panics about forms of violent crime and violent behaviour, such as 'garrotting' in the 1850s and early 1860s and young 'hooligans' at the turn of the century. The appalling but isolated murders attributed to Jack the Ripper in the autumn of 1888 also created a nationwide scare, thanks, according to a head of the Metropolitan Police CID, to "the sensation-mongers of the newspaper press who fostered the belief that life in London was no longer safe, and that no woman ought to venture abroad in the streets after nightfall".'

Results Plus

Watch out!

Many students assume that crime figures can be used to show crime trends. Don't assume it's that simple! An increase in convictions can be evidence that law enforcement and detection had improved rather than evidence that there were more crimes.

Activities

These questions are exam-style questions for those students studying Unit 3D 'The work of the historian'.

1 Study Sources A and B.

   What impression do you get from these sources about the level of violent crime in London?

2 Study Source C.

   What impression of the level of threat posed by violent criminals has the artist tried to create?

   Explain your answer, using Source C.

3 Study Sources B and C.

   How reliable an impression of the dangers posed by garrotters do you think is provided by Source C?

   Explain your answer, using Sources B and C.

4 Study Sources B and E.

   Which would be more useful to a historian trying to explain fear of violent crime in Victorian London?

5 Sources D and E state that violent crime in the 19th century was actually falling, despite a high level of fear.

   Explain the difficulties a historian has in finding out about the amount of crime. Suggest sources a historian could use in order to discover whether the crime rate was falling.

3.1 Changes in policing and combating crime since 1900

Learning outcomes

By the end of this topic you should be able to:

- describe ways in which policing and detecting crime has changed since 1900 and explain why
- assess the impact of these changes on crime prevention and detection.

Activities

1 Which of the changes in the technology of policing described opposite do you think is most important in:
(a) *deterring* crime, (b) *detecting* crime? Explain your answers.

2 Look at Sources A and B. What can you learn from these about the impact of new technology on policing in the 20th century?

The impact of technology on fighting crime

- **Fingerprinting:** everyone's fingerprints are different. The fingerprint department of New Scotland Yard was set up in 1901. In 1995 a National Automatic Fingerprint Identification System allows every police force in England and Wales to compare fingerprints found at crime scenes.

- **Radios:** modern communication makes it easier to report issues and call for back-up. The police first used radios in 1910 and the technology continues to develop today.

- **Computers:** sorting information, finding patterns and matching evidence saves a huge amount of police time and can spot information people would miss. The Police National Computer was introduced in 1980 and holds records on 25 million people. It can alert police to criminals who have committed crimes similar to ones being investigated. Also, monitoring websites and emails allows the police to hunt for those planning acts of terrorism.

- **DNA evidence:** can be discovered from tiny quantities of hair, skin and blood. This can be used to identify both victims and criminals. In 1995 the DNA National Database Library was set up.

- **Cars and motorbikes:** greater mobility allows police to get to crime scenes faster. One of the biggest changes of the later 20th century was taking police off the beat and putting them in cars.

- **CCTV:** allows people's behaviour on the streets to be checked. CCTV security cameras were first used by the police during the IRA bombing campaign of the 1970s. CCTV cameras can be viewed as events are happening, but the cameras also record events that enable criminals to be captured at a later date.

Source A: Radio-equipped motor-cycle patrols in 1931.

Community policing in the 20th and 21st centuries

Modern policing is not just about technology. The setting up of Neighbourhood Watch schemes involve local people in crime prevention. This is comparable with ways used to combat crime in the 15th century, which made local communities responsible for the behaviour of their neighbours and reporting crime. The difference is that the modern scheme is completely voluntary.

Source B: First use of miniature police radios in 1963.

DOWN NOW TO 7½oz

THE HIDDEN VOICE–
in yesterday's crowds

TOWERING head and shoulders above the crowd outside St. Paul's yesterday, a stern-faced police constable appeared to be talking into his hand.

Crowds, who pressed forward to catch a glimpse of the VIPs arriving for the memorial service to President Kennedy, wondered if the P.-c. was holding a conversation with his four fingers and thumb.

Only the closest spotted the tiny, two-way radio held in his palm. It linked him with a traffic and crowd operations room in the City of London's police headquarters, in nearby Old Jewry.

From his spot in the midst of the heaving crowd, the policeman was summoning reinforcements to control the swaying spectators, who looked like getting out of hand.

In the ops. room, messages went out to a dozen other P.-c.s to battle their way into the area and the messages, which crackled out of the top pockets of the constables through the tiny radios, were individually acknowledged and the reinforcements moved in.

The miniature two-way radio was having its first real work-out in crowd and traffic control in the City of London, famed for its pageantry and State occasions.

Fighting

Tomorrow, the two-way radio will be fighting crime as it links policemen on the beat with their operational headquarters.

And in the next year, if top Home Office planners have their way, every policeman in Britain will be equipped with this instant line of communication to summon help, report crime or be available for a sudden switch to trouble areas.

A City of London police spokesman told me yesterday: "We have been experimenting with these personal radios for the last six months.

"They weigh only 7½oz. and fit into the breast pocket of our police patrolmen. We have 30 radios in use now and we intend to extend them to cover every P.-c. on our force."

They operate on an ultra-high-frequency channel, independent of the normal VHF wavelengths used by squad cars.

Lancashire Constabulary, always the pioneer in modern police methods, have placed a £67,500 order for 500 pocket radios for their constables, perfected by their own technicians. These operate over a five-mile radius.

Instantly

Experiments are going ahead in Bc. and Durham to equip forces there with this instant link which will make police boxes as out-of-date as the bull's-eye lantern.

Chief Constables throughout the country are enthusiastic about this system after witnessing a demonstration of a 15-mile radius radio at last year's annual convention.

A senior Scotland Yard administrative officer told me yesterday: "These personal radios could lead to a complete revolution in the beat system."

PETER DUFFY

In London yesterday a P.-c. gets out his tiny two-way radio to call for reinforcements.

Challenges facing policing in the 21st century

Peel created a police force that had an immediate presence on the streets, although modern police often feel they are more effective in cars. However, many people want to feel the reassurance of a police officer walking down their street as a deterrent to crime.

The threat of terrorism from groups such as the IRA in the 20th century and Al-Qaeda in the 21st century means that police share intelligence across the world. Also, armed police often look like soldiers. This was exactly what Peel tried to avoid.

The complexity of international crimes such as terrorism and fraud mean that there are questions about (a) how long the police should hold a suspect before they charge them and (b) whether ordinary people on a jury can always understand the evidence.

Activities

3 'Modern technology has transformed the job of the police force.' How far do you agree with this view? Use evidence from this unit to back up your opinion.

Challenge

4 Why might Sir Robert Peel have been unhappy with some developments in modern policing? Think about the kind of police force he intended and the way he organised its work, then compare this to modern developments.

Summary

- Modern technology has had a great impact on policing since 1900.
- Some aspects of police work still require the presence of the police that Peel would recognise from 1829.
- Combating threats such as terrorism causes a difficult balance between people's rights and people's safety.

3.2 Changing patterns of crime since 1900

Learning outcomes

By the end of this topic you should be able to:

- identify examples of changing definitions of crime since 1900 and why these have occurred
- describe ways in which patterns of crime have changed since 1900 and explain why these changes have happened.

Before...

By the late 19th century, despite newspaper reports that suggested the opposite, violent crime figures were declining.

Changing definitions of crime

Changes in society mean that definitions of crime can change over time.

Racist crime has become an issue as Britain has become a more multicultural country.

As women's and children's rights have improved, the law has changed to punish domestic violence.

Conscientious objectors were treated as criminals because they refused to fight in war.

Changing definitions of crime

Men accused of cowardice were shot in the First World War.

Increased use of motor cars has led to punishment of those who drive badly. New laws have been created that cover speeding limits in different areas, alcohol levels and driving, and types of driving considered dangerous.

Source A: Following the inquiry into the murder of Stephen Lawrence, this drawing appeared in the *Evening Standard* on 25 February 1999.

The Stephen Lawrence Inquiry

The Stephen Lawrence Inquiry of 1999 highlighted the terrible nature of racist crime. Stephen Lawrence was a young black man brutally murdered in 1993 by a white gang. The inquiry accused the police of 'institutional racism' in not putting sufficient effort into catching the murderers and in the way it treated Stephen's family. A copy of the Stephen Lawrence Inquiry can be found by going to www.heinemann.co.uk/hotlinks (express code 4417P) and clicking on the appropriate link.

Activities

1   Look at each of the changes in attitudes towards what is a crime in the spider diagram opposite. Explain (a) which ones were temporary changes and (b) which ones were part of longer lasting changes in society since 1900. Explain how you decided.

Changing attitudes towards what constitutes crime

Ideas about what constitutes a crime change over time. This is nothing new. We have seen how begging became a crime in the 16th century and how workers organising themselves to protect their wages and conditions became a crime in the early 19th century. Since 1900, there have been examples of similar changes in what is regarded as criminal activity. Some of these did not turn into permanent attitudes. Others were part of long-term changes in society.

Conscientious objection

In 1916 conscription was introduced that forced men to join the military in World War One. Those who refused became criminals (unless they were able to persuade a special tribunal that they should be exempt from military service). Once these men refused an order, such as to put on a uniform, they were court-martialled. They could receive sentences of up to two years' imprisonment.

Cowardice in the face of the enemy

Deserting your post has always been a crime in the military, but the terrible effects of modern war on soldiers in World War One meant that many of those who deserted their posts were suffering from a form of mental illness called shell shock. Today, such men would receive mental health care but between 1914 and 1918, 306 'deserters' were executed.

Traffic crime

Speeding, dangerous driving and using mobile phones while driving are all crimes today but were not before the 20th century, due to the absence of motor cars or mobile phones. Changes in technology caused this change as it has been thought necessary to control how we use this technology in order to protect people. Changes in society have made drink-driving and dangerous speeding socially unacceptable – although some drivers still resent speed cameras if they feel there is no danger to others if they exceed the limit.

Race crime

The Race Relations Act (1968) made it illegal to refuse housing, employment or public services to a person on the grounds of colour, race, ethnic or national origins. Discrimination therefore became illegal. Continued racial abuse and violence towards members of minority groups has meant that 'racially motivated crime' is now explicitly punished whereas, before the middle of the 20th century, the racist motivation of such crime would not have been considered seriously.

Domestic violence

Violence in the home has often been ignored unless the crime involved murder or serious assault. It was often a hidden crime, but during the 20th century there has been increased awareness of both the rights of women and children, and the levels of violence that exist in some homes. This has led to changes in the law, which have been designed to punish such violence.

Activities

2 Choose one of the examples above and explain how it shows changing attitudes towards what is regarded as 'crime'.

3 How is this similar to any other changes in the definitions of crime you have studied from an earlier period of history? Explain what this earlier example was and how it is similar.

4 What is the meaning of Source A? How does it show changing attitudes towards racist crime in the late 20th century?

DAILY EXPRESS

ONLY 40p

THE WORLD'S GREATEST NEWSPAPER

www.express.co.uk

THURSDAY APRIL 17, 2008 40p

YOUTH, 17 CHARGED WITH RHYS MURDER
SEE PAGE 10

Shannon's mother on trial with man accused of kidnap
SEE PAGE 7

IMMIGRANTS BRING MORE CRIME

By **Tom Whitehead** Home Affairs Editor

IMMIGRATION from Eastern Europe has led to a huge surge in crime, police chiefs will tell the Home Secretary today.

The hundreds of thousands of migrants who have flocked to Britain in recent years have had a significant impact on communities and have placed fresh demands on policing, a review has found.

Pressure on police resources has soared while a lack of criminal intelligence from Poland and its neighbours has left the UK vulnerable to criminal gangs.

The damning report will be presented to Jacqui Smith in a key meeting, at which many chief constables will demand extra funds to cope with the effects of Labour's open-door policy.

It comes a day after leaked extracts from the study were used to create a positive image with claims that migration has not caused crime waves. But the full report, seen by the Daily Express, paints

TURN TO PAGE 6

Picture: MARK LARKIN

Dame Helen Mirren names Britain's largest liner yesterday SEE PAGE 3

QUEEN HELEN AHOY

Crime trends since 1900

- Crime has increased since 1900.

- The prison population has increased since 1900.

- However, the percentage of women in prison has fallen since 1900.

- Since 1992 the level of crime has fallen.

- Some newspapers, though, give the impression that the level of crime is increasing.

Activities

5 Carry out a survey of friends and neighbours. Do they think levels of crime are increasing/decreasing? Which types of crime do they think are increasing/decreasing? What experiences do they personally have as victims of crime? Report to your class on your findings and compare your results.

The increase in levels of crime since 1900

Has crime increased since 1900? The answer is clearly 'yes'. The number of offences per thousand people in the population in 1900 was 2.4 and in 1997 the figure was 89.1. A rising trend in reported crime began in 1954, when the figure was 9.7. This increase in crime in the 20th century is reflected in increases in the prison population. Previous periods of time such as the 18th century have also seen increases in the prison population due to changes in society and law enforcement.

Why have these changes occurred?

It is clear that historians cannot simply assume that problems in the economy lead to increased crime. From 1901 to 1914 the crime trend was downwards despite increasing unemployment and industrial unrest. In addition, the prison population was at its lowest during the high unemployment of the 1930s. So, poverty on its own does not explain increases in crime. However, between 1946 and 1986 the average male prison population increased. This was at a time when living standards were going up. Perhaps the answer lies in people having less respect for others and for authority, and a consumer culture where people assume they can get what they want and are more likely to commit crime if they cannot. Better law enforcement and sentencing can result in more prison sentences (such as for burglary and car crime). Similar changes in policing and sentencing led to increased numbers of prisoners during the time period 1750–1850.

Other factors affect the appearance of other crimes in national statistics. The increased influence of the Women's Movement since the late 1960s has increased awareness of violence towards women. The same increased awareness has led to an increase in the reports of rape since this crime is now more sensitively handled by the police and courts. Also, better law enforcement increases the numbers of criminals punished.

The fall in crime rates since 1992

Reported crime was at its highest in 1992. Since then the amount of crimes committed appears to have gone down. This may be because a greater number of criminals have been imprisoned due to changes in court sentencing and because increased prosperity has discouraged some forms of property crime.

Why do many people think levels of crime are increasing?

First, many people's experience of crime comes from burglary and street violence, and these have increased. Second, newspapers give a great deal of coverage to crime and make people think that the crime rate is worse than it really is.

Activities

6 (a) What happened to levels of crime between 1900 and 1992? (b) What has happened since 1992?

7 Look at Source B. What impression does this give you of the place of crime within British society today? How does this source help to explain why many people fear that crime is increasing? Does this amount of fear agree with the crime statistics? Explain your answer.

8 What explanations can you suggest for the increase in crime between 1900 and 1992?

Challenge

9 Why can it be difficult to give a simple answer about levels of crime in society today?

For discussion

10 Are newspapers to blame for the fear of crime in modern British society?

Summary

- Since 1900 a number of new definitions of crime have led to the punishment of different groups of people who would not have been punished before.

- Since 1900 crime overall has increased. However, since 1992 there has been a fall in the levels of crime, according to official statistics.

- The way that some newspapers report crime suggests that crime is increasing when overall it has been falling since 1992.

3.3 Why was capital punishment abolished?

Learning outcomes

By the end of this topic you should be able to:

● identify the arguments used in the 1950s for and against capital punishment

● explain what events led to its eventual abolition.

Timeline of events leading to the abolition of capital punishment

1908 People under 16 no longer hanged.

1933 People under 18 no longer hanged.

1950 Timothy Evans executed for the murder of his wife.

1953 Derek Bentley to be hanged at Wandsworth Prison.

1955 Ruth Ellis, the last woman hanged in the UK.

1964 Last executions: Peter Anthony Allen and Gwynne Owen Evans.

1965 Capital punishment for murder cases suspended for five years.

1969 Abolition of capital punishment for murder.

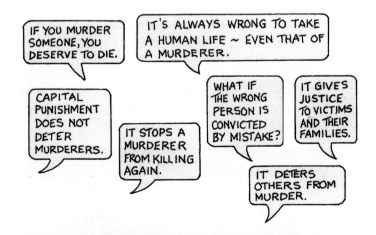

IF YOU MURDER SOMEONE, YOU DESERVE TO DIE.

IT'S ALWAYS WRONG TO TAKE A HUMAN LIFE ~ EVEN THAT OF A MURDERER.

CAPITAL PUNISHMENT DOES NOT DETER MURDERERS.

IT STOPS A MURDERER FROM KILLING AGAIN.

WHAT IF THE WRONG PERSON IS CONVICTED BY MISTAKE?

IT GIVES JUSTICE TO VICTIMS AND THEIR FAMILIES.

IT DETERS OTHERS FROM MURDER.

Activities

1 Sort the statements above into arguments for and against capital punishment.

2 How could you use the events on the timeline above to explain that the abolition of capital punishment was not a sudden decision made in 1969?

Source A: Cartoon from 1962. It suggests that, with politicians and judges opposing the use of capital punishment, only those who wanted to 'put the clock back' (and opposed progress) were in favour of it.

LISTEN TO INFORMED OPINION, SIR, NOT TO A LOT OF WOOLLY DO-GOODERS!

Changes in the law after 1900

In 1908 the execution of under 16s stopped. In 1933, persons under 18 (at the time they committed the crime) would not be hanged. Changes in society meant that more people thought executing another person was wrong. This is very different from attitudes in earlier periods of history.

The impact of controversial executions

A number of important criminal cases caused public opinion to become more critical of the use of capital punishment.

Timothy Evans, 1950

Evans was hanged for killing his wife and baby. Later evidence revealed that Mrs Evans (and at least five other women) had really been murdered by a man named Christie, who lived in the same flats as the Evans family. Evans was posthumously pardoned in 1966.

Derek Bentley, 1953

Derek Bentley (aged 19) and Christopher Craig (aged 16) broke into a London warehouse in 1952. Craig shot and killed a policeman. Derek Bentley had serious learning difficulties and a mental age of 11. Both men were found guilty of murder but only Bentley was executed because Craig was under 18 years old. He was posthumously pardoned in 1998.

Ruth Ellis, 1955

This became a very controversial case because she had suffered violent abuse from the boyfriend that she shot. However, the killing was planned and Ruth was sane. As a result, the jury had no choice but to find her guilty, but the case made people very unhappy that no other sentence seemed available. She was the last woman to be hanged in the UK.

The abolition of capital punishment

In 1957 a change in the law limited the death sentence to five types of murder.

In 1965 another change in the law abolished capital punishment but allowed another vote on it five years later. However, treason, piracy with violence and arson in the royal dockyards remained capital crimes. In December 1969 parliament confirmed the abolition of capital punishment for murder. Sources B and C show part of the parliamentary debate.

Explain why Derek Bentley's execution was important in changing attitudes to capital punishment. (9 marks)

■ **Basic, Level 1 (1–3 marks)**
Answer gives a reason but with little detail.

● **Good, Level 2 (4–6 marks)**
Answer gives details about public protests and Derek Bentley's execution, but does not explain fully its importance.

▲ **Excellent, Level 3 (7–9 marks)**
Adds to Level 2 an explanation to show that public opinion became more critical of the use of capital punishment because of concern over Bentley's execution.

3 Using the information on pages 38 and 39, make an ideas map (like the one on page 34) to explain why the death penalty ended in the 20th century.

Challenge

4 Changes in attitudes in society can lead to changes in the law in a number of areas. Carry out research on how such changes have led to new laws concerning sex discrimination.

Source B: James Callaghan, Labour Government Home Secretary, in a speech to parliament on 16 December 1969, in the debate on the final abolition of capital punishment.

'These figures show that the murder rate is not soaring as a result of the abolition of capital punishment but remains remarkably stable.'

Source C: The Conservative Opposition Spokesman on Home Affairs, Quintin Hogg, in the same debate. He believed that murders had happened because violent criminals no longer feared being hanged for murder.

'There are people dead today [because of murderers] who might have been alive if the law had been different.'

After…

In 1971 arson in the royal dockyards stopped being a capital offence. In 1998 high treason and piracy with violence stopped being capital crimes. In 1999 the Home Secretary (Jack Straw) signed the 6th protocol of the European Convention on Human Rights, formally abolishing the death penalty in the UK.

Summary

- During the 20th century a number of changes to the law restricted the use of capital punishment.
- A number of controversial executions added to the calls to abolish it.
- Capital punishment for murder was finally abolished in 1969 and completely in 1998.

3.4 Changing punishments in the 20th century

Learning outcomes

By the end of this topic you should be able to:

- describe some of the functions of prisons and how these changed over the last century
- consider alternatives to prison in the 21st century.

Before...

Before the mid-20th century prison was often seen as the most important way to respond to crime because it was thought to both punish the criminal and make them less likely to offend again. It was also thought that treatment in prison should be harsh.

Changes in prisons in the 20th century

In 1922 the Separate System of confinement of prisoners (see pages 28–29) was abolished. Prison Officers (called 'warders' since 1919) were given training on how to re-educate prisoners. In 1933 the first 'open prison' was established. With greater freedom, these were to be used for less dangerous criminals and those close to release. Since 1907 probation officers have worked with offenders to monitor their behaviour; putting offenders 'on probation' instead of in prison was a big change in the approach to punishment. For more dangerous prisoners, 'high security' prisons have been established with increased security.

In 1948 the Criminal Justice Act abolished hard labour and corporal punishment. It also set up new Detention Centres for some young criminals.

Activities

1 What are prisons for? How many purposes can you come up with?

Concern at rising crime rates soon led to these offering harsher treatment than in the borstals of the 1930s.

Women and the changing prison system

Recent years have seen a dramatic rise in the numbers of women being sent to prison, but there are still many more male prisoners than female ones. About 6 per cent of the prison population is female, and often the crimes that send women to prison are connected with poverty, drug dependence and mental health problems. Statistics for female prisoners show that they are more likely than not to use hard drugs, have mental health problems and to have suffered abuse in the past. There are a large number of self-harm incidents in women's prisons.

Women have always committed much less crime than men. It has been estimated, for example, that between 12 and 20 per cent of all those transported to America and Australia were women, usually for crimes to do with theft or prostitution – both of which can have a direct connection to poverty. British society has always punished women much more heavily for 'immoral behaviour' than men, which seems somewhat hypocritical when it is men who create the demand for prostitutes and who also often take the money the women earn.

Currently, there are 14 women's prisons in England, with 4 female juvenile units and 7 'mother and baby' units. The everyday routine of prison life is similar for male and female prisoners, but women's jails do have some differences, for example in the health services that are provided and in the amount of time women are allowed to spend with their children.

Children and the changing prison system

In 1908 prisons called Borstals were set up to hold young criminals, reflecting a recognition that young people should have separate prisons to stop them being influenced by older criminals. Concentrating on hard work and education, they were initially quite successful in reducing the number of re-offenders. However in recent years Young Offenders Institutions in the UK have recorded rising levels of violent behaviour.

Prison reform campaigners criticise the UK government for locking up more children than other European countries, and at a younger age. Campaign groups point to the evidence that children in prison are likely to have come from very disadvantaged backgrounds, to have mental health problems and to have been excluded from school. Re-offending rates are also very high for this group. However, governments remain under pressure to be seen 'doing something' about crime.

ResultsPlus

Top tip!

Always give an example when you make a statement about a change. Don't just say 'the treatment of young offenders changed in the 20th century'. Add 'for example "Borstals" were set up in 1908. They concentrated less on punishment and more on rehabilitation and reform through education.'

Alternatives to prison

As a result of changing attitudes, modern courts do not always use prison. Community sentences may include attending drug or alcohol treatment programmes, work on community projects or charity work. This may involve some criminals having to meet victims of their crimes. Programmes such as these aim to make offenders understand the effects of their crimes. They are often combined with measures to tackle issues such as illiteracy, unemployment or homelessness that might lead them to re-offend. Since 1998 magistrates' courts can issue an anti-social behaviour order (ASBO) banning a person from committing offending behaviour. New technology such as electronic tagging has provided an alternative to prison, while still restricting the movements of offenders.

Source A: Justice Minister, David Hanson, reported the following in July 2008.

'Prison is necessary to punish and reform offenders and protect the public from the most serious, dangerous and persistent offenders… But it is not necessarily the best route for less serious offenders who may lose their job, their accommodation and their family ties after a short period of imprisonment. Putting offenders through tough community sentences can often be more effective in reducing re-offending than a short spell in prison and the research published today shows the British public want rehabilitation of offenders at the heart of our justice system, and they want what works to cut crime.'

Activities

2 In what ways does prison punish an offender?

3 Describe alternatives to prison that might be used by the modern courts.

4 How have official attitudes towards the use of prisons changed since the mid-19th century? Look back at topic 2.6 and compare what you have learned with Source A.

Challenge

'Restorative justice' is another community sentence. This provides an opportunity for victims and criminals to discuss an offence and how to repair the harm done. This can help offenders to recognise the effects of their actions and encourage them to set things right.

5 What advantages and disadvantages can you see in getting criminals and victims to meet to discuss the effects of crime? Do you think Howard and Fry would have approved of it?

Summary

- Prisons now exist to fulfil a number of functions.
- Alternatives to prison are increasingly used and are often thought to be the most effective way to rehabilitate non-violent criminals.

3.5 How new are 'new crimes'?

42

Learning outcomes

By the end of this topic you should be able to:

● identify 'new crimes' found in the UK in the 21st century and compare these with crimes in the past

● decide how 'new' these 'new crimes' really are.

Modern crimes?

Possible new crimes and their links to older forms of crime	
Old	**New**
Selling of poor girls into prostitution was a problem in 19th-century cities.	People trafficking. Many people from Eastern Europe and less economically developed countries are illegally brought to the UK and forced to work for low wages, or no wages at all.
In the 18th century organised criminal gangs smuggled goods.	Drug smuggling is a multi-million pound industry.
Impersonating another person to steal their money is an old crime, as is tricking money out of a person.	Computer crime is often used to commit fraud.
Street robbery and other forms of street crime have been a problem for centuries.	Street crime and anti-social behaviour causes great concern in many towns and cities.

Source A: *Daily Mail* cartoon, September 2002, showing street crime.

'Hey! You can't steal that! It contains statistics proving that street crime is down!'

Source B: An illustration from Pierce Egan's *Life in London* 1821, showing a man being robbed by a gang in the street.

Activities

1 Explain how certain crimes look like 'new crimes', then explain how often 'old crimes' have been quite similar.

2 Which of these 'new crimes' do you think is most different from crimes committed in the past? Explain the reasons for your decision.

ResultsPlus
Watch out!

Students often assume that crimes using new technology are new crimes. Many of them are actually still examples of fraud or theft – not new crimes at all.

International smuggling

New

In 2007–08 Customs seized 41,422 kilograms of illegal drugs (such as heroin). These drugs were worth many millions of pounds. A government study in 1999 found that since 1997, about £5 billion in taxes had been lost because of cigarettes brought illegally into the UK.

Old

Look back at topic 2.3 to remind yourself of the goods smuggled by organised gangs of criminals in the 18th century. Even today, while most people would strongly disapprove of smuggling illegal drugs, they may be less concerned about smuggling cigarettes and alcohol. This is an '18th-century attitude'!

People trafficking

New

According to UK Government statistics, about 4,000 women and children are trafficked into prostitution in the UK at any one time. Hundreds of men, women and children are trafficked into forced labour, including domestic slavery, farmwork, building work and food processing.

Old

The term the 'white slave trade' was first used in the 1830s and referred to female prostitution and especially child prostitution. In 1885 William Stead (a newspaper editor) and Bramwell Booth of the Salvation Army joined forces to expose the trade in child prostitutes.

Computer crime

New

Computer technology can be used to carry out many types of crime:

- storage of illegal images on a hard disk instead of in print

- illegal downloads of music and other forms of piracy

- 'phishing' – using spoof emails to direct a computer user to a fraudulent website in order to illegally transfer money, passwords or credit card details

- 'hacking' (gaining unauthorised access to a computer), or writing a 'virus' (malicious software) to delete stored data.

Old

Some of these crimes are old crimes using new technology: storing illegal images, harassing someone, impersonating another person, illegally taking money by fraud. Some, such as 'hacking', are new crimes, made possible by the new technologies.

There are totally 'new crimes'. Speeding is an example due to new technology. Changing attitudes can cause new definitions of crime. An example is driving while using a mobile phone, since people have realised over time that it leads to accidents.

Activities

3 Many 'new crimes' are actually 'old crimes' done in different ways. Choose two of the 21st-century crimes described in this topic and, for each example, explain how far they support this point of view.

Challenge

4 Identify some genuinely 'new crimes' – activities you can be fined or sent to prison for in the 21st century that you couldn't have been in the 19th century.

Summary

- A number of crimes appear to be 'new crimes' but many of these are, in reality, 'old crimes' using different methods.

- There are new opportunities for crime provided by new technology. Changing attitudes change definitions of crime.

3.6 The work of the historian: why is preventing suicide bombings such a challenge to the police in the 21st century?

Four suicide bombers attacked central London on Thursday, 7 July 2005. These attacks killed 52 people and injured more than 770. The attacks hit the transport system just as the morning rush-hour was coming to an end. Three bombs went off at about 8.50 am on three Underground trains just outside Liverpool Street and Edgware Road stations, and on another train travelling between King's Cross and Russell Square. The fourth (and final) explosion was about an hour later, on a double-decker bus in Tavistock Square, not far from King's Cross station.

This was the first time that suicide bombers had struck in London. These attacks followed those in New York on 11 September 2001 (almost four years earlier). Although there had been terrorist attacks from Irish groups over many years, these suicide attacks were a very different challenge to the police and security services.

Source A: From a radio advertisement put out by the Metropolitan Police in February 2008, encouraging Londoners to report suspicious behaviour that might lead the police to terrorists.

'How d'you tell the difference between someone just videoing a crowded place and someone who's checking it out for a terrorist attack?

How can you tell if someone's buying unusual quantities of stuff for a good reason or if they're planning to make a bomb?

What's the difference between someone just hanging around and someone behaving suspiciously? How can you tell if they're a normal everyday person, or a terrorist?'

Source B: Poster produced by the Metropolitan Police in February 2008, as part of their counter-terrorism advertising campaign.

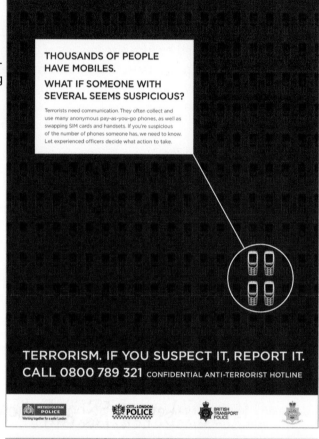

THOUSANDS OF PEOPLE HAVE MOBILES.

WHAT IF SOMEONE WITH SEVERAL SEEMS SUSPICIOUS?

Terrorists need communication. They often collect and use many anonymous pay-as-you-go phones, as well as swapping SIM cards and handsets. If you're suspicious of the number of phones someone has, we need to know. Let experienced officers decide what action to take.

TERRORISM. IF YOU SUSPECT IT, REPORT IT.
CALL 0800 789 321 CONFIDENTIAL ANTI-TERRORIST HOTLINE

METROPOLITAN POLICE · CITY OF LONDON POLICE · BRITISH TRANSPORT POLICE

Source C: A modern cartoonist's impression of the difficulty of identifying terrorists.

Source D: Assistant Commissioner Peter Clarke, Head of Counter Terrorism Command, April 2007.

'[It was thought that] The experience gained during some 30 years of an Irish terrorist campaign would have equipped us for the new challenges presented by Al Qaeda… To an extent this is true but only to an extent… [The Irish attacks were] carried out by terrorists in tightly knit networks who were desperate to avoid capture and certainly had no wish to die. The use of warnings restricted the carnage, dreadful though it was.'

Source F: Deputy Assistant Commissioner Barbara Wilding on when she became chairperson of the Metropolitan Police suicide bomber working party. Quoted in the *Guardian* newspaper in 2006.

'It was within about 10 days of 9/11 [2001] that I was asked to review strategy and come up with a plan,' says Wilding. 'With Irish terrorism there always tended to be a warning and an escape plan. The IRA didn't want to die. They wanted to leave their bomb and live. With suicide terrorism, the target was innocent civilians. There was no escape plan at all. To live was to fail.'

Source E: From *The British War on Terror: Terrorism and Counterterrorism on the Home Front Since 9–11* by Steve Hewitt, 2007.

'Another obvious difference between traditional terrorism as experienced in the United Kingdom and the more modern version is suicide bombing. Terrorism related to Ireland did not involve suicide bombing nor did those carrying out attacks seek massive and indiscriminate casualties.'

Source G: From *Why Terrorism Works: Understanding the Threat, Responding to the Challenge* by A.M. Dershowitz, 2003.

'These loose knit groups are especially difficult to combat because they often employ suicidal terrorists who are not subject to the usual deterrent threat – death or other severe punishment. They also lack a "return address" – a known location where they can be attacked without civilian casualties.'

Activities

1   Study Sources A and B.

    What can you learn from Sources A and B about the difficulties facing the police in identifying modern terrorists?

2   Study Source C.

    What impression of the difficulty of identifying modern terrorists has the artist tried to create?

    Explain your answer, using Source C.

3   Study Sources A, D and E.

    How much of the police officer's account in Source D do you think is a reliable explanation of why the police have found it so difficult to combat suicide bombers?

    Explain your answer, using Sources A, D and E.

4   Study Sources B and F.

    Which of Sources B and F would be more useful in identifying the problems the police face in preparing for the challenge presented by suicide bombers?

    Explain your answer, using Sources B and F.

5   Study Source G and use your own knowledge of the work of the historian.

    Source G suggests that modern terrorist groups are harder to combat than groups the police have faced in the past.

    Explain the difficulties the historian faces in proving this and suggest other research the historian could do to check this claim.

45

Summary: Crime and punishment

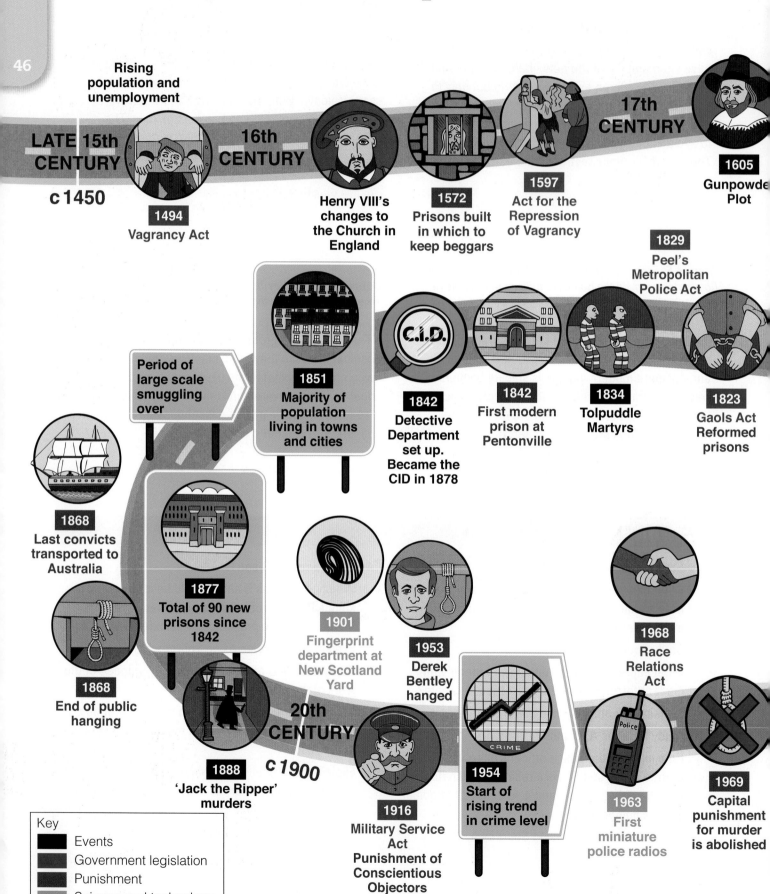

LATE 15th CENTURY

c 1450

Rising population and unemployment

1494
Vagrancy Act

16th CENTURY

Henry VIII's changes to the Church in England

1572
Prisons built in which to keep beggars

1597
Act for the Repression of Vagrancy

17th CENTURY

1605
Gunpowder Plot

1829
Peel's Metropolitan Police Act

Period of large scale smuggling over

1851
Majority of population living in towns and cities

1842
Detective Department set up. Became the CID in 1878

1842
First modern prison at Pentonville

1834
Tolpuddle Martyrs

1823
Gaols Act Reformed prisons

1868
Last convicts transported to Australia

1877
Total of 90 new prisons since 1842

1901
Fingerprint department at New Scotland Yard

1953
Derek Bentley hanged

1968
Race Relations Act

1868
End of public hanging

1888
'Jack the Ripper' murders

20th CENTURY

c 1900

1916
Military Service Act Punishment of Conscientious Objectors

1954
Start of rising trend in crime level

1963
First miniature police radios

1969
Capital punishment for murder is abolished

Key
- Events
- Government legislation
- Punishment
- Science and technology

46

1671
Game Act

Start of 'Bloody Code' aimed at deterring crime

1749
Bow Street Runners

1776
End of transportation to America

1777
Howard publishes *The State of Prisons*

18th CENTURY

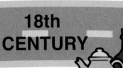

Increased taxes on tea and brandy

1725
Hanging of Jonathan Wild

1735–1749
The Hawkhurst Gang control south coast smuggling

Start of rapid industrial growth

1787
Transportation *First Fleet* sails to Australia

1823
Peel reduces death penalty by over 100 offences

1819
Peterloo Massacre

1818
Elizabeth Fry tours prisons

1815
Death penalty for 225 offences

19th CENTURY

Widespread smuggling of French goods

1988
First murderer convicted using DNA evidence

1995
DNA National Database Library set up

1998
First ASBOs

2008
Prison population 82,319

1970s
Changes in court sentences: probation, community service, etc.

1992
Levels of crime start falling

1998
Prison population 65,300, 4 times that of 1901

21st CENTURY

2005
London Tube and bus bombings

2008
Rate of crime declined 10% in 2006–2007

Quick quiz

1 Which of these punishments was rarely used in the Middle Ages: (a) imprisonment, (b) whipping, (c) branding?

2 What was a 'sturdy beggar'? Why were they in trouble in the 16th century?

3 Give the name of one prison reformer.

4 When was the last person hanged in the UK?

5 What was the 'Bloody Code'?

6 When did transportation to America stop and why?

7 What does ASBO stand for?

8 What does 'crime rate' mean?

9 Who were the Hawkhurst Gang?

10 Name the first of the new-style Victorian prisons built after 1840. Would prison reformers have been pleased with how prisoners were treated in it?

Support activity

1 Think back over what you have learnt about crime and punishment since 1450:

a) What would you say was the biggest difference in policing between 1450 and today? Are there any similarities?

b) What would you say was the biggest difference in punishing crime between 1450 and today? Are there any similarities?

Find out more

For more information about the subjects covered in this section, go to www.heinemann.co.uk/hotlinks (express code 4417P) and click on the appropriate link.

- Crime and punishment: this provides access to a wide range of evidence relating to crime and punishment from the National Archives.

- Criminal trials: this provides a searchable collection of information on 197,745 criminal trials held at London's central criminal court between 1674 and 1913. It is a fascinating way to explore the evidence for the changing treatment of crime during this period.

- Jack the Ripper: this provides a huge amount of information on Jack the Ripper and the state of London's East End in the 1880s.

- 18th-century crime reports: this provides access to early 18th-century crime reports in contemporary newspapers.

- Beggars: this provides a good insight into the treatment of beggars and the poor.

- Capital punishment: this provides a very detailed source for capital punishment in the UK.

- Smuggling: this provides a detailed history of smuggling and smugglers.

- History of the police: this provides a very good overview of the history of the police force.

A good account of the transportation system is given in the book *The Fatal Shore* by Robert Hughes (1987).

Checklist

Read through the following list and evaluate how well you have done each of the following.

- Explored examples of how definitions of 'crime' change over time and why this happens.
- Looked at changing causes of crime and why these causes are sometimes different in different time-periods.
- Considered why ideas about appropriate levels of punishment change (the rise of the Bloody Code, abolition of capital punishment).
- Explained how and why policing has changed since 1450. What similarities and differences are there over time?
- Explored how different groups have different experiences of the law.
- Considered the role individuals play in causing change to happen. You will also have seen how their impact links with wider changes going on in their society.
- Analysed key 'turning points' in changing experiences of crime, punishment and policing.

Student tips

Remember, when you are revising crime since 1450, to identify whether what you are learning is part of the changing punishment of crime, or the policing/detection of crime. These are two connected but different areas. They often develop at different rates at different times. Sometimes the main focus in a time-period can be on one area, rather than on the other (e.g., punishment of crime was a major feature in the mid-18th century, improved policing in the 1830s).

Student tips

Remember to look carefully for the reasons why changes occur in responses of the law to crime. These changes sometimes take place because of the particular impact of an individual, sometimes due to actions of a number of people acting together, sometimes due to wider ranging social trends. Usually these different factors combine in order to cause change to occur. But it is helpful to recognise the different cause factors that lead to a development.

Introduction to the exam

When you are examined on this topic you will find three general types of question.

In question 1 (4 marks) you will be given two sources and asked to use them to explain something about developments in crime and punishment since 1450 (e.g. change or continuity in a particular area).

In question 2 (9 marks) you will be given a piece of information and asked to explain its importance in the history of crime and punishment (e.g. the name of a prison reformer or the name of a person whose hanging was controversial). You will have to make a choice of one out of two to write about.

You will have a choice of question 3 or 4 (12 marks). You will be given a piece of information (e.g. a picture or some bullet points) and asked to use it to help you explain a development in crime and punishment (e.g. a picture of a beggar being whipped and a question about why beggars were so harshly treated in the 16th century).

On the next pages you will find some examples of exam questions along with some examples of student answers and examiners' comments.

Mini exam paper

1 What can you learn from Sources A and B about continuity in approaches to punishment between the 17th and 21st centuries? Explain your answer using these sources. **(4 marks)**

Source A: Punishment in the stocks (17th century).

Source B: Justice Minister, David Hanson, reported the following in July 2008.

Putting offenders through tough community sentences can often be more effective in reducing re-offending than a short spell in prison and the research published today shows the British public want rehabilitation of offenders at the heart of our justice system, and they want what works to cut crime.

2 The boxes below show two important individuals. Choose ONE individual and explain why that person was important in changing attitudes towards punishment. **(9 marks)**

Elizabeth Fry and Newgate prison

Derek Bentley and capital punishment

3 Why were vagabonds and sturdy beggars treated so harshly in the Tudor period? **(12 marks)**

The following information may help you with your answer.

A 16th-century drawing of a beggar being whipped through the streets.

This is important. You won't get any credit for writing about both. Spend some time jotting down some notes and thinking about which you could write the best answer on before you start your answer.

This question focuses on causation. So, do not just describe what you know, say what caused this to happen.

This is the content focus. What do these terms mean? What do you know about them? Why are they important in the study of crime and punishment?

This is the time-period focus. Keep your answer focused only on the Tudor period, in the 16th century.

Use this to get started, but you must bring in your own knowledge in order to build on the memory prompt that you get from this picture.

Don't just describe the picture. Use it to explain briefly how sturdy beggars were treated and – most importantly – why this took place. What caused people to treat beggars in this way?

Choose ONE individual and explain why that person was important in changing attitudes towards punishment. (9 marks)

Elizabeth Fry and Newgate prison	Derek Bentley and capital punishment

Student answer

Elizabeth Fry was a Quaker who thought it was wrong to treat prisoners in a brutal way. She visited Newgate prison and showed kindness to the prisoners. She taught people to read and sew and encouraged the government to take action to improve conditions in English prisons. She got people talking about prison reform and how prisons should be improved.

Examiner comments

This answer neither states when Elizabeth Fry was active nor explains what the attitude was towards prisons before she challenged it. As a result this makes it harder to assess what change she brought about. The answer also does not identify other factors which affected her influence or any limits on her effects. As a result the answer is mostly descriptive.

Extract from an improved student answer

The Christian Quaker Elizabeth Fry challenged the idea that prisoners should be kept in appalling conditions as punishment. Instead, she believed better treatment could reform prisoners and rehabilitate them to return to society as better citizens. In Newgate Prison she set up education classes and in 1825 published her ideas on improving prisons. She was important because some of her ideas were taken up by Robert Peel, who reformed prisons. But the new prisons – though cleaner and less crowded – still aimed at harsh punishment (like solitary confinement) which Fry would not have approved of.

Why were vagabonds and sturdy beggars treated so harshly in the Tudor period? (12 marks)

The following information may help you with your answer (see image and caption on page 50).

Student answer

In this picture a person is being whipped through the streets because he is poor. The kind of people doing it and watching it seem well dressed and this reminds us that it was usually well-off people who were behind this way of treating the poor. There is also a person being hanged outside the town, which shows that this was also done to people who were found guilty of serious crimes. This happened because well-off people were frightened of the beggars on the streets, and wanted to punish them to get rid of them and to stop them from begging.

Examiner comments

This answer spends too much time describing the picture and does not really say what kind of people were treated this way. The word 'poor' is too vague. Not all poor people were treated this way. It does not say *why* these kinds of punishments happened – what was going on to make better-off people anxious about beggars and what they hoped to achieve from these types of punishments. There is a mention of capital punishment, which is not really relevant to this answer (unless the student shows that they know that this could be the punishment if a person kept on begging).

Extract from an improved student answer

'Sturdy beggars' were treated harshly in the Tudor period. Such beggars were called 'sturdy beggars' because it was thought they were fit enough to work but were refusing to. People also felt that 'sturdy beggars' needed harsh treatment to make them work! Such people were considered a threat because it was thought they had chosen their life of begging. This worried many wealthy people as they feared that wandering beggars were likely to commit crimes. The increase in the number of beggars in the Tudor period was actually caused by factors such as the increase in sheep farming, but it created a moral panic in a society where people were expected to know their place in the community.

4.1 Crime and punishment from Roman Britain to c1450: introduction

Introduction

In this topic, you will be looking at crime and punishment in Britain from the 1st century CE through to the end of the Middle Ages in approximately 1450. The period of study covers more than a thousand years. Some things changed very little in this period, others changed a great deal.

Aims and outcomes

In particular, you will be examining the degree of continuity and change in three different aspects of crime and punishment:

- what activities were defined as 'crimes' by the authorities, and by communities, across these centuries
- how law was enforced and different crimes punished
- how attitudes in society, including ideas about religion, have influenced approaches to crime and punishment.

Source A: An extract from the Institutes of Justinian, 533 CE. They are outlining the power men had over women and children under Roman law.

> The offspring, then, of you and your wife is in your power, and so too is that of your son and his wife… But the offspring of your daughter is not in your power, but in that of its own father. Women are in the power of their husbands, or if they have none, of their fathers…

The nature of criminal activity

Robbery or theft was one activity that was defined as criminal across this period. It was considered serious as it was seen as breaking the king's (or government's) peace.

Source B: Illustrations from a manuscript showing some aspects of law and order in the reign of King John in the 13th century.

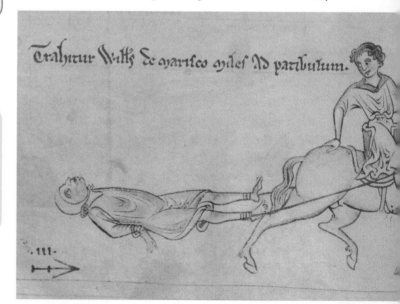

Timeline

43	c410	c410–1066	663	871–899
The Romans invade Britain	Collapse of Roman Empire; withdrawal from Britain	Anglo-Saxon England	Synod of Whitby establishes the authority of the Church of Rome in England	Reign of Alfred the Great in Wessex

The nature of punishment and law enforcement

Hanging for crimes such as theft was the usual punishment during the Middle Ages.

Social attitudes to crime and punishment

An illustration of the execution of a heretic. These were people who refused to accept the main beliefs and practices of the Roman Catholic Church, which was the only religion allowed in Britain in the Middle Ages. It shows the importance of the Church and religious beliefs in crime and punishment in this period.

Activity

1   Get into groups of four or five.

Use the sources and information on pages 52 and 53.

(a) What ideas about law and order are similar and which are different compared with ours today?

(b) How many of the law and order problems are similar to ours today?

(c) What are the main differences in law and order problems?

954	1066	1154–1189	1215	1361
England becomes a united country	Norman Conquest	Reign of Henry II – including the Assize of Clarendon, 1166	The use of Trial by Ordeal condemned by the Catholic Church	Justices of the Peace Act

4.2 Attitudes to crime and punishment

Learning outcomes

By the end of this topic you should be able to:

- describe general attitudes to crime and punishment throughout the period c43–c1450
- identify some of the continuities and changes in attitudes.

Ideas about what is a 'crime' and how criminals should be punished sometimes change as societies change. A 'crime' is an act that is against the law of the country in which you live. This raises many questions, which we will look at in this topic. What was classed as a crime and why? How did this change over time? How did attitudes to crime affect the way criminals were punished? How did punishment change over time?

Attitudes to crime – continuities

Many of the crimes themselves and ideas about what was a criminal activity and how it should be punished remained constant through the period.

- The beliefs and attitudes about crime and punishment found in different societies mainly reflected those of the more powerful groups or classes who had the power to make and enforce the law. Their interests and concerns were often given special protection by the laws they passed.
- Social attitudes to crime and the punishment of criminals for most of the period from the Romans to the end of the Middle Ages changed very little.
- Individuals were usually held to be totally responsible for their criminal actions, no matter what their own circumstances were. For example, economic problems were never taken into account. Unlike 21st-century Britain, these societies did not try to understand the causes of crime in order to think about how crime could be prevented.

- One aspect of attitudes to crime and punishment that remained largely constant from Roman times through to the Middle Ages concerns women. Women were seen as inferior and were treated unequally by the law. They were often punished more harshly than men for similar crimes.
- What counted as a crime remained much the same throughout the whole period. Acts of violence against individuals were classed as crimes. There are some differences within these 'crimes' from today, though. For example, killing a slave in Roman Britain was not classed as murder. Theft – stealing money or property – continued to be the most common crime. Just as today, this varied from petty theft, such as stealing an item of food, to violent robbery of money or valuables.

ResultsPlus
Watch out!

Students often only focus on change and forget about continuity – it's important to remember what stayed the same as well.

Attitudes to punishment – continuity and change

The key aims of punishment also remained fairly consistent for most of this period. They were:

- Deterrence – punishments were made deliberately harsh in order to try to stop others doing the same thing.
- Revenge – wanting the criminals to suffer for their actions.

In addition, the authorities throughout this period used punishments that were cheap to carry out and that did not need to be run by complex organisations.

Source A: Robbery or theft was one activity that was defined as criminal across this period. Highway robbery was considered serious, as it was seen as breaking the king's (or government's) peace.

Activities

In pairs:

1 Jot down some ideas about what was made a 'crime' in Roman Britain – remember to think about who was making the laws.

2 Discuss some of the similarities and differences that you can see between attitudes to crime and punishment in Britain before 1066 and today. For example, how would a mentally ill person who had committed a crime be treated today compared to how they might have been treated then?

There were some changes, however.

- From the time of the Anglo-Saxons, the influence of the Christian Church resulted in a slightly less brutal approach to punishment. For example, there was less use of the death penalty.
- The idea of restitution rather than retribution became more important during the later Anglo-Saxon period. The *wergeld* or *wirgild* was a system based on the payment of money compensation to the victim.

Summary

Attitudes to crime and punishment can change when societies change. There was also much continuity in the period from Roman Britain to the end of the Middle Ages.

4.3 Society, law and order in Roman Britain

Learning outcomes

By the end of this topic you should be able to:

- explain the nature of Roman society and how this affected attitudes to crime
- describe how the law was enforced in Roman Britain.

Activities

1 Today in the UK, there are many laws regarding the family – divorce laws or domestic violence laws, for example. Make a list of any you can think of and then mark which ones you think would not exist in Roman Britain.

Before...

Before the Romans conquered Britain, the different Celtic tribes had their own legal systems.

Roman society

Roman Britain, like the rest of the Roman Empire, was hierarchical – meaning that different people had power over others. At the top of society were wealthy families who owned property and slaves. At the bottom of society were the slaves themselves. There were groups in between. Roman Britain was also a patriarchal society. This means that it was run by men. The father was the head of the family and his wife, children and slaves (if owned) were under his control and had to obey him. It was up to the father how his family were treated.

The types of crime under the Romans were partly linked to the great inequalities that existed in the Roman Empire. While some people were extremely wealthy, there were many who lived in great poverty. At times, there were also severe food shortages if harvests were bad. The government did very little to deal with such problems. As a result, there were many who were desperate enough to risk breaking the law. The temptation to resort to crime was made greater by the fact that there was no proper police force to prevent crime or arrest suspected criminals.

Roman law

After Rome conquered Britain, its strong central government and good system of communication throughout the empire meant that Roman laws were introduced and enforced in Britain. So for the first time Britain had a centralised and common system of law and law enforcement. Roman law and principles were more rational than earlier legal systems, and were not based on religion.

The Roman emperors had the power to make and enforce laws. However, large sections of society did believe that law should be based on certain principles. These included:

- the right of every person to know what the laws were
- the right of a defendant to know any charges being brought against them
- the idea of innocence until proven guilty
- the right to present evidence in court
- the right to a fair trial in a court, which should be run according to rules that were open and fair to those accused of breaking the law.

The belief that people should know what the laws were led to Roman law being written down and made public. The twelve tablets of the laws of Rome were carved onto metal sheets and displayed in town centres five hundred years before the Romans invaded Britain. They remained the basic principle of Roman law, even when there were changes as time went on. In the century after the Romans left Britain, the Emperor Justinian created a Code that recorded and summarised Roman law. We can see from the *Institutes of Justinian* how much continuity there was throughout the Roman period with the first principles.

Source A: An extract from the *Institutes of Justinian*, 533 CE.

> 'Governors often condemn people to be held in prison or kept in chains, but they are not supposed to do so, for such penalties are forbidden; prisons ought to be for detaining men [for trial], not for punishing them.'

Activities

2 Are there any similarities that you can spot between the Roman attitudes towards law and justice and those of today?

3 What do Sources A and B show about the role of the emperor in Roman law?

Law enforcement in Roman Britain

Britain was a province of the Roman Empire. The provincial governor dealt with all important cases, while officials known as magistrates dealt with minor cases in small local courts. The Romans did not believe that large sums of money should be spent either on a professional police force or on punishing criminals. Therefore, the role of controlling the province was undertaken by the Roman legions stationed in Britain. If someone felt they had been robbed, they had to take the suspect to the local centurion who then decided, on the evidence provided, whether the case should be tried. As there was no proper police force, victims of crime were responsible for collecting evidence and, sometimes, for taking the suspect to court.

Source B: A mosaic showing the kind of punishment imposed on Christians who refused to obey the emperor's laws concerning religion.

Summary

- In the Roman period, Britain had a centralised legal system for the first time.
- Britain was controlled by the governor who heard legal cases, but there was no proper police force.
- There were criminal courts.

4.4 Crimes and punishments in Roman Britain

58

What were the main types of crime?

The most frequent crimes were lesser ones such as small-scale theft or selling under-weight bread. Apart from this petty theft and stealing of low-value items, other crimes such as burglaries and street-crimes involving robbery or simple street violence were also common. General riots at games, chariot races and gladiatorial contests also took place from time to time.

Source A: An extract from some observations about crime made by Juvenal, a Roman poet and author, writing in approximately 100 CE.

'Nor are these the only terrors. When your house is shut, when bar and chain have made fast your shop and all is silent, you will be robbed by a burglar or perhaps a cut-throat will do for you with cold steel.'

Source B: A fresco, or wall painting, showing the serious fighting that broke out between rival supporters at the gladiatorial games in Pompeii in 59 CE.

The most serious crimes

As you will see across many of the periods that you will study, the crimes viewed as the most serious were those that threatened the authority of those in power.

Rebellion

As the Roman Empire conquered so many different countries and peoples, rebellions often took place. The most severe and gruesome punishments were reserved for those who rebelled or plotted against the emperor. In Britain, the most serious rebellion against the Romans was in 60 CE, when the Iceni in East Anglia rose under their queen, Boudicca.

Religious non-conformity

While people conquered by the Romans were allowed to continue worshipping their own gods, they also had to worship the emperor as part of the official civic religion. When Christians refused to do this, they were severely punished.

Types of punishment under the Romans

Because there was no proper police force to prevent crime, the main method used by the Romans was to make punishments harsh, in the belief this would deter criminals. Prisons were not used to punish those found guilty of crime. Instead, they were used to detain accused people waiting for their case to come to court. Harsh physical punishments and executions were frequent and carried out in public as a deterrent.

Punishments often depended on who the criminal was. Men were punished differently from women, slaves differently from freedmen and Roman citizens differently from non-citizens. For example, slaves convicted of theft were executed whereas a free person would be flogged. Wealthy criminals were often able to escape harsh physical punishments by paying compensation to their victims.

Crimes	Punishments
Minor crimes (e.g. petty theft)	• Flogging (being whipped) • Beating • Financial penalties (being forced to repay the cost of goods stolen or damaged, for example)
Major crimes (e.g. mugging)	• Amputation of limbs
More serious crimes (murder, arson, libel and slander)	• Execution (by various methods) • Exile (only available for the upper classes)
Most serious crimes (such as refusing to accept the authority of the emperor)	• Execution by crucifixion or being thrown to the lions • Being forced to become a gladiator

Source C: An engraving showing Christians being eaten by wild animals in the arena (3rd century CE).

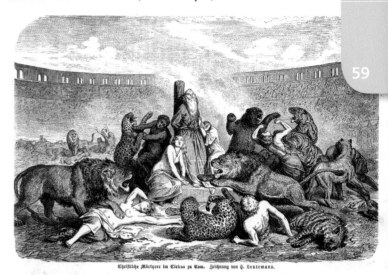

Chriſtliche Märtyrer im Cirkus zu Rom. Zeichnung von H. Leutemann.

Source D: Extracts from the *Twelve Tables* on the laws dealing with damage to persons and property (451 BCE).

'For the fracture of a bone (or a tooth) of a freeman, the penalty is 300 asses; in the case of a slave, 150. For any injury whatsoever committed upon another, 25 asses…

[A person setting fire to] a house or of a haystack near a house, if acting intentionally and of sound mind, shall be bound, scourged [whipped] and put to death by fire… .'

Activities

1 What similarities and differences can you find between violent crime in Roman times and today?

2 What can you learn from Source C about the nature of Roman punishment?

3 Why were groups such as Christians punished so harshly?

Summary

- The most common crime in Roman times was petty theft.
- The most serious crimes were against the emperor or Roman authority.
- Punishments were often severe and violent. The death penalty was used frequently.

4.5 Anglo-Saxon society and law and order

Learning outcomes

By the end of this topic you should be able to:

- outline how Anglo-Saxon society made laws and kept law and order
- explain the role of the local community and the king in law making and law enforcement
- show what was similar to and what was different from Roman times.

Activities

1 In groups, discuss (a) the importance in Anglo-Saxon society of the local community and family and (b) the influence of the Christian Church. Discuss how you think these new influences impacted on what laws were passed, how law was enforced and what punishments were carried out. Over the next few pages you will find out if you are right.

What happened to law and order when the Romans left?

When the Roman Empire collapsed in the 5th century CE, their unified system of law and order largely collapsed too. North German tribes such as the Angles, Saxons and Jutes took over. They used much more basic, small-scale and local systems. Then, much of eastern and northern England was conquered and ruled by the Danes and Vikings who made their own laws. This meant that once again there were many different systems of law across Britain. However, as the authority of the later Anglo-Saxon kings grew, in the 9th and 10th centuries, there was acceptance of the increasing role of the king in making laws and enforcing them, especially as England developed into a single kingdom.

What were the most important features of Anglo-Saxon society?

How did Anglo-Saxon society differ from Roman society and how did this affect crime and punishment? The Anglo-Saxon period saw two main changes from Roman times:

- the importance of local community and family
- the influence of the Christian Church.

The importance of family: the blood feud

A major difference between the early Anglo-Saxon and Roman societies was the importance of kinship and family ties. This meant that loyalty to your family was highly prized. This had a huge impact on crime and punishment as family groups stuck together in support of their kin. There was no police force or Roman army to enforce the law, so in general it was left to those who had been the victims of crime to punish the wrongdoer themselves. This meant that the victim or the victim's family had the right to take revenge on the person who had done harm – including the right to kill the accused person or a member of their family. However, this method often led to long-running family feuds and violence, which is why it became known as the blood feud. Later on, it was seen as causing as much violence as it was supposed to punish. It also made it difficult for the less powerful or less violent people to get justice.

Collective responsibility

Tithings

Although the time of the blood feud ended by the 9th century, later Anglo-Saxon law was still essentially based on the local community. By 1000, an elaborate legal system had been built up, based on shires and hundreds (containing 100 peasant farms). To enforce the law, the men had to belong to a 'tithing' (a group of ten free males). The tithing acted as a system of collective responsibility. If one of the ten committed a crime, the others had to make sure he appeared in court – or pay a fine themselves. The tithing also had to alert the rest of the hundred to any crime by raising the 'hue and cry'. Again, loyalty to your community was the key, so it was the duty of each tithing to arrest criminals. However, often the victims of crime were expected to find the criminals themselves.

The law and the role of the king

Throughout the Anglo-Saxon years the role of the king in law making and enforcement grew. All kings had advisers who could guide them, but that did not mean they had to follow their advice. The king was in overall charge of the law. He had the responsibility to ensure that the 'king's peace' was kept so that his subjects could live and travel around without fear. Offences against the king's peace, such as robbing a traveller, would be punished harshly (see Source A on page 55).

Some later Anglo-Saxon kings drew up Codes of Law. The most important of these was issued by King Alfred of Wessex in the 9th century. However, these were not as complete as the Roman *Institutes of Justinian* (see page 57) because most of Anglo-Saxon law was unwritten – it was based on custom.

Later, Anglo-Saxon kings tried to reduce the violence of the blood feud with the wergeld (wirgild). This was a system based on the payment of money compensation. Wergeld was paid if someone was killed or murdered, and a botgeld (botgild) was payable for injuries. The rates varied according to the social rank of the person killed or injured.

Source A: An 11th-century manuscript showing a Saxon king with his advisers and the hanging of a man found guilty of breaking the king's law. This shows the importance of the king in law making and enforcement.

Source B: Extracts from a 9th-century Anglo-Saxon scale of payments (wergeld) to be paid by the guilty person to the victim's family.

For killing a choerl or labourer – 200 shillings
For killing a bishop – 1200 shillings
For killing an archbishop – 3600 shillings

Summary

- Anglo-Saxon law was more localised than Roman law as Britain was split up into different kingdoms for much of the period.
- The role of the local community grew, as did the role of the king during the period.

4.6 Anglo-Saxon society: the influence of the Church

The role of the Christian Church in society grew after the Synod of Whitby in 663 when Anglo-Saxon kings converted to Christianity. This led to big changes in several respects: first, what was classified as a crime and second how people were punished for crimes. It was also the beginning of the idea of God acting as a judge on who was innocent or guilty.

Source A: Some of the laws from the code issued by Alfred the Great, 871–899.

> 6 If anyone steals anything in church he is to pay the normal fine and then have his hand struck off.
>
> 9 If a pregnant woman is murdered, the killer is to pay the full wergild for the woman and half for the child.
>
> 40 If anyone neglects the rules of the Church in Lent he is to pay 120 shillings.

Activities

1 Source A shows connections between religion, the Church and crime. Is this different from or similar to Roman times? How?

2 What new attitude to punishment is revealed by Source B?

New laws?

The increasing influence of the Church meant that new laws were brought in. An example can be seen in Source A where people who did not abide by the Church rules in Lent would be fined.

Church influences on punishments

The beliefs of the Christian Church had a considerable effect on punishment. The death penalty, which had been important in the Roman system, was rarely used (except for the most serious crimes or for re-offenders). Instead, mutilations became more common, as this, they believed, gave the guilty the chance to repent and so save their soul. This introduced a new idea about the purpose of punishment – the idea that offenders could be reformed. However, this remained a minority view for many centuries.

Anglo-Saxon crime and punishments

Despite the changes that we have looked at in Anglo-Saxon society, the types of crime appear to have remained much the same, with small-scale theft continuing to be the most common.

Source B: An extract from the code of laws drawn up in the early 11th century for Ethelred and Cnut by Archbishop Wulfstan. It shows the views of the Church on capital punishment just before the Norman Conquest.

> 'Christian men shall not be condemned to death for all too little; but one shall determine lenient punishments for the benefit of the people, and not destroy for a little matter God's own handiwork…'

There were two main ways in which Anglo-Saxon law decided on the guilt of an individual accused of an offence:

- **Trial by the community**
  The guilt or innocence was decided in a court by a jury made up of local men who knew the people involved.

- **Trial by ordeal**
  If the jury simply could not agree, then Anglo-Saxon law relied on trial by ordeal, which would reveal the judgement of God on the case.

In a trial by ordeal, the Church was responsible for the trial process. The most common forms were ordeal by hot water (the accused plunged his arm into boiling water) and ordeal by fire (the accused had to walk three paces carrying a red hot iron). In each case, God's judgement was revealed by the priest after inspecting the hand three days later. If the wounds had not festered, the accused was innocent. Two other forms of ordeal were (a) by cold water (mainly used for slaves – if the accused sank in a pool he was innocent); (b) by sacrament (only used for priests who were declared innocent if they could eat the holy bread without choking).

Source C: Trial by ordeal in Anglo-Saxon times, which would reveal the judgement of God on the case.

If someone was found guilty by one of these two main methods, they were then condemned by the court to the punishment set down by law. The most common form of punishment was the payment of compensation and fines. However, more serious crimes were treated more harshly.

Crimes	Punishments
Minor crimes (e.g. petty theft)	• Fines
Major crimes or repeat offences	• Fines • Confiscation of property • Beatings, floggings
Stealing	• Cutting off hands or feet
Slander	• Cutting off tongue
More serious crimes (murder, arson)	• Execution (most commonly hanging, but occasionally beheading, burning, stoning or drowning)
Most serious crimes (e.g. treason against the king)	• Execution by beheading, burning or hanging

Activities

3 What similarities and differences can you see between Roman and Anglo-Saxon methods of punishment for certain crimes of violence?

Summary

- The Anglo-Saxon period sees the beginning of the influence of the Church in what was classified as a crime and how people were punished.
- The death penalty was less common than in Roman times as it was believed that criminals should be given a chance to repent and save their souls.

4.7 The impact of the Norman Conquest

Learning outcomes

By the end of this topic you should be able to:

- describe the 'new' crimes brought in under the Norman rulers
- explain why these new crimes were created.

Before...

By the time of the Norman Conquest in 1066, England had a reasonably unified system of law and law enforcement, with the Church and the king playing leading roles.

Norman society

There was not such a large difference between Norman and Anglo-Saxon society as there had been between Roman and Anglo-Saxon society, and many aspects of crime and punishment remained the same. However, there were some important differences. The Normans brought customs and ideas with them from Normandy when they invaded England. These can be summarised as:

- The power of the king – the role of the king increased.
- Centrality of the Church – religion became even more important.

Preventing challenge to authority

The Norman invaders were outnumbered by about 300 to 1 by the Anglo-Saxon population of England. The first task was to ensure acceptance of Norman authority in the face of resistance and even outright rebellion. The most serious rebellions were between 1069 and 1070, in the south-west, on the Welsh borders and especially in East Anglia and the North of England.

Source A: A declaration made by William I in 1070, following a series of rebellions.

'I will that all the men whom I have brought with me, or who have come after me [from Normandy] shall be protected by my peace [mund] and shall live in quiet. And if one of them is killed, his murderer's lord shall capture the slayer within five days if he can; but if not, he shall start to pay me forty-six marks of silver so long as his possessions last. But when they are exhausted, the whole hundred in which the slaying occurred shall pay in common what remains.'

Activities

1 What new crime is Source A attempting to deal with?
2 What evidence is there in Source A of both change and continuity with Anglo-Saxon approaches to law enforcement?

This Anglo-Saxon resentment of, and resistance to, the Norman Conquest led to the creation of a 'new crime' of killing a Norman. This is an example of how rulers make laws to protect themselves and others in authority.

Forest Laws

William I promised to uphold Anglo-Saxon laws (see page 66), but some aspects of law, and hence crime, did change after 1066. The most important changes introduced by William were the result of his new Forest Laws. He declared that about 30 per cent of England would be protected Royal Forests controlled by a introduced new Forest Laws, which introduced new crimes and the punishments for them. These were very harsh and even if deer were eating their crops, it was now a crime for people

Source B: An illustration of the punishment in the stocks of a monk and a nun for committing the moral crime of having had sexual relations with each other.

to kill them. As well as covering large areas of woodlands, the Forest Laws also included farms and villages, and many of the more remote places of England. Punishments for breaking these new laws were very cruel.

William I loved deer hunting, but the Forest Laws did more than allow the king and his successors to hunt freely. They were an important extension of royal authority in the most strategic and valuable regions:

- a large network of forest officials policed the laws of the forest, adding to the king's control
- fines and special forest taxes added to the monarch's wealth and hence his strength
- the Forest Laws were designed to add to the king's ability to maintain law and order in lawless areas.

Crime and the Church

Finally, as the Normans gave the Church even more involvement and power with regard to the law, there was more prosecution of what were religious or moral crimes. William I set up Church Courts for such crimes, and the number of moral crimes dealt with increased. These included adultery, sex before marriage, as well as not following all the rites and practices of the Church. William also used the courts to control the behaviour of priests. If they were found guilty of moral crimes, they too were punished. The influence of the Church in law enforcement is later shown by the ending of trial by ordeal in 1215 when the Church refused to administer oaths.

Activities

3 What can you learn from Source B about the role of the Church in crime and punishment?

4 Make a chart in two columns headed 'New crimes' and 'Similar crimes'. Use the information in this section to complete column 1. What do you think will go in column 2?

Summary

- The Norman invasion brought some new laws into action based on Norman beliefs of the importance of the Church and morality.
- The Norman invasion also brought some new laws into action based on protecting the power of the new king and ruling families.

4.8 Continuity in Norman law enforcement

Learning outcomes

By the end of this topic you should be able to:

- describe the continuity in law enforcement from Anglo-Saxons to Normans
- explain the changes made by the Normans to law enforcement.

As we have seen, several changes concerning law enforcement and punishment took place under the Normans. However, many aspects of Anglo-Saxon law remained almost unchanged.

How much continuity was there?

The role of the king

Norman law was based on the idea of the 'mund', an area of land around every man's home in which peace and order should be allowed to exist. This was very similar to the 'king's peace' that gradually grew up under the Anglo-Saxon kings. After 1066, because the king owned the whole country, his 'mund' covered everybody. The idea of the king's 'mund' meant that William was responsible for law and order throughout his kingdom.

So, with regard to the importance of the king in making law and in enforcing it on the whole country, law under the Normans was similar to that established in Anglo-Saxon England, although William's authority was greater.

Local systems of law enforcement

Many aspects of the Anglo-Saxon system fitted in quite easily with Norman practices. In particular, the reliance on shire courts and sheriffs for the maintenance of law and order continued, although the Normans used the term 'county' instead of shire. The local law enforcement role of the hundreds also continued almost unchanged for many years. Tithings, the system of hue and cry, and trial by ordeal, all continued. Like the Anglo-Saxons, the Normans had no police force.

Source A: An extract from a royal proclamation issued by William I; it was later re-issued by Henry I, who ruled from 1100 to 1035. Edward the Confessor had been the Anglo-Saxon king from 1042 to 1066.

> 'This also I command and will, that all shall have and keep the law of King Edward [the Confessor] … together with those additions which I have established for the benefit of the English people.'

Source B: An extract from orders sent by Henry I to the important men of Worcestershire in 1100, shortly after he became king.

> 'Know that I grant and order that henceforth my shire courts and hundred courts shall meet in the same places and at the same terms as they were accustomed to do in the time of King Edward, and not otherwise.'

Activities

1 'Sources A and B show continuity between Anglo-Saxon and early Norman law.' Explain two ways in which the sources support this statement.

2 How far do these sources show that law enforcement changed after the Norman Conquest?

ResultsPlus
Top tip!

Students who get the best answers remember to support their statements and opinions with examples.

Source C: A medieval drawing of a trial by combat.

What changes did Norman law bring to law enforcement?

Some aspects of law enforcement changed after 1066. One minor change that took place was the introduction of a new method of trial by ordeal. This was trial by combat, which demonstrates the importance of warfare in Norman society. It had long been a Norman custom and was added by William to the existing Anglo-Saxon traditions. The Normans believed that God would show guilt through the result of combat between the accused and accuser. An invalid or a woman could be represented by an appointed 'champion'. Although not a common method of settling disputes, trial by combat continued well into the Middle Ages, outlasting the other trials by ordeal until it too was abolished in the late Middle Ages.

Local law enforcement

Most ordinary people's experience of the law continued to be with their local manor court where the lord acted as judge, and the jury was made up of the heads of the tithings. County courts were set up to deal with more serious crimes.

Towns also came under the king's mund. To set up a new town, people had to get a charter from the king. Such a charter gave freedom from the local manorial court, and instead allowed towns to have their own borough court.

Activities

3 How was the method of trial by combat shown in Source C similar to the ordeals used under Anglo-Saxon law before 1066?

Summary

There was much continuity to the law after the Norman Conquest.

4.9 Norman attitudes and punishments

Learning outcomes

By the end of this topic you should be able to:

● explain why there was an increase in corporal and capital punishment under the Normans

● describe the attitudes that influenced Norman approaches to punishment.

Increase in capital punishment

We have already seen how the new Norman rulers faced much resistance from the Anglo-Saxons. Harsh punishments were seen as a way of frightening people so they did not challenge authority. There was an increase in the number of people given the death penalty. However, it was not just crimes against Norman authority that received harsh punishments. Physical punishments (mutilations and amputations) and executions became more common and the idea of paying compensation to victims began to decline. In particular, hanging was used for a wide range of offences, including theft and arson, as well as murder. Some of the harshest punishments were given to those breaking the new Forest Laws. Punishments were carried out in public as a deterrent – in order to scare those who watched – and to show the community that the law was enforced.

For minor crimes, the main punishments remained basically the same as those used in the Anglo-Saxon period – fines, whipping, or public humiliation in the stocks or pillory. The purpose of this last method of punishment was to expose those in the stocks to public ridicule and anger.

Activities

1 Compare the type and frequency of Norman punishments with those that occurred in Anglo-Saxon and Roman times. Which societies are most similar? Why?

Norman crimes and punishments

Crimes	Punishments
Minor crimes (e.g. petty theft)	• Fines • Stocks or pillory
Major crimes	• Beatings and floggings • Amputation of hands, arms etc.
Serious crimes (murder, arson) or repeat offences	• Execution (most commonly hanging, but occasionally beheading, burning, stoning or drowning)
Most serious crimes (rebellion, heresy)	• Execution by beheading, burning or hanging

Source A: The number of hangings increased under the Normans. Hanging for crimes such as theft was a usual punishment at this time.

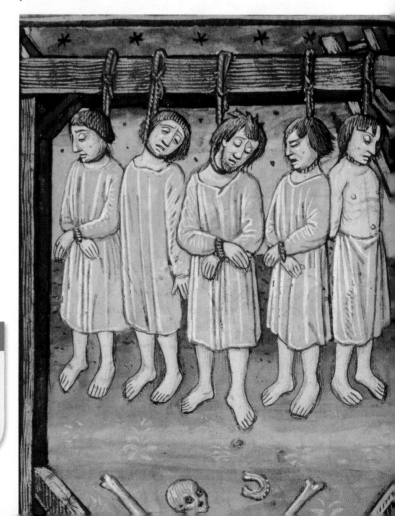

The Church's influence

The Church continued in its attempts to introduce a new aspect into law enforcement – that punishment should also try to save the soul of the criminal and reform them. This approach was strengthened when William I set up Church Courts to deal with moral crimes (see page 65). The importance of the Church continued to increase as both the taking of oaths and trial by ordeal were the main methods of deciding a person's guilt or innocence.

There were also two ways in which the influence of the Church sometimes protected the guilty from royal justice.

- **Benefit of clergy:** priests could only be tried by Church courts, which had no power to use the death penalty. It was originally assumed that only priests would be educated enough to read, but many wrongdoers escaped by learning by heart the passage from the Bible (nicknamed the neck verse) used for the test.

- **Right of sanctuary:** a criminal who could get to the sanctuary of a church could not be arrested. If he confessed his crime, he would be allowed to leave the country.

Activities

2 Create a presentation explaining the influence of the Church on crime and punishment after the Norman Conquest. You must include:
  - How religion affected what was classed as a crime.
  - How religion affected punishment.
  - The role of the Church in enforcing and punishing criminals.

  Do some of your own research and use the information on this page and page 65 to help you.

Source B: An extract from the account of a 14th-century coroner, which shows how the right of sanctuary operated. Palmer was allowed to leave the country rather than face punishment.

'On 24 May 1379, William Palmer, who was outlawed for the death of Thomas Wydenhale, was arrested and put in the stocks. But he broke them and fled to Leighton Buzzard church and stayed there for 13 days. On 6 June, he confessed to William Fancott, county coroner, that he had murdered Thomas on 5 June 1370. He sought the sanctuary of the Church and it was granted to him.'

Results**Plus**
Build better answers

How much did the Norman Conquest change approaches to law and order in England? (16 marks)

■ **Basic, Level 1 (1–4 marks)**
These answers usually make general comments without detail – for example, punishments were harsher.

● **Good, Level 2 (5–8 marks)**
Good answers provide more detail, for example, about the harshness of the Forest Laws.

▲ **Better, Level 3 (9–12 marks)**
These answers will make comparisons to show the similarity or difference with the Anglo-Saxon approach – for example, showing the similarity in the continued role of the Church and the difference in the new harshness of approach to punishment.

▲ **Excellent, Level 4 (13–16 marks)**
These also weigh up the amount of change overall, having given examples of a range of similarities and differences.

Summary

- There was an increase in corporal and capital punishment under the Normans.
- Severe methods were used to prevent challenges to authority, but the influence of the Church sometimes allowed wrongdoers to escape punishment.

4.10 A new legal system in the later Middle Ages

Learning outcomes

By the end of this topic you should be able to:

- describe the changes made regarding law enforcement under Henry II
- explain the developments that occurred during the latter part of the Middle Ages.

Before...

For a long time after 1066, Anglo-Saxon and Norman law continued to operate side by side, although it was Norman law that dominated. However, during a civil war that lasted from 1135 to 1154, law and order broke down. This illustrates the importance of strong government in the maintenance of law and order.

A new system of 'royal justice' after 1154

In 1154, at the end of the civil war, Henry II became king. His priority was to restore the authority of the king. He had to tackle the problem of the 'over-mighty' subjects – powerful individuals such as sheriffs or great nobles who felt strong enough to ignore the law and decisions of the courts. One of the ways he did this was to update and draw together the Anglo-Saxon, Norman and royal laws in the Constitutions of Clarendon, 1164. In this way he created the basis of the English Common Law

(the one we have today). For the first time since the Romans, England had a system of unified law that was the same throughout the land.

Henry also reformed the system of law enforcement to make the king more powerful.

Source A: A 15th-century illustration showing the court of King's Bench, first set up by Henry II. The people on the left are the jury.

Activities

1. Why might Henry II have disliked the power of the Church?

2. Compile a table of similarities and differences between the influence of religion on crime and punishment in late medieval times and:
   - Roman times
   - Anglo-Saxon times
   - Norman times
   - today.

Use of juries

Juries of presentment were set up. Known as 'grand juries', these had been used before, but Henry II made them a more regular and important part of the legal system. They had to report breaches of the law to the sheriff. They did not decide guilt or innocence. In Henry II's reign, trial by ordeal was still common, but he encouraged the use of new 'petty juries' (so-called in order to distinguish them from the more important grand juries). Increasingly, they were used to decide on the guilt or innocence of accused people.

Royal writs

To make sure powerful sheriffs enforced the king's law, writs (the king's instructions) were written and sent.

The court of king's bench

The most serious criminal cases were dealt with by the king's court (a new court in London) and not in the local courts.

Travelling justices in eyre

England was divided into six 'eyres' or circuits and royal judges travelled around to hear the legal cases using the English Common Law.

Law enforcement after 1154

County gaols

All counties now had their own prisons where accused people were keep before the judge arrived to try their case.

Church justice

Henry also attempted to reduce the legal rights and privileges of the Church such as separate courts, sanctuary and benefit of clergy (see page 69). However, the Church's power was so great that Henry was forced to allow Church courts to continue. In fact, after 1154 the Church played an even greater role in the English legal system. Not only did it provide educated men to record laws, draw up writs and act as judges, it also influenced the laws that were made and how those found guilty were punished (see pages 72–73).

Developments after Henry II

The work begun by Henry II to extend the royal system of justice and law enforcement was continued after his death in 1189 (see pages 72–77). During the Middle Ages the organisation of law enforcement improved.

- In the reign of King Richard I, a new legal official – the coroner – was introduced. He dealt with all suspicious deaths.

- The number of petty juries was further increased and by the end of the 14th century, trial by jury was the normal method of deciding guilt.

- In 1361, the Justices of the Peace Act was passed. JPs were local landowners who were given the power to hear less serious crimes. They held their own 'Quarter Sessions' courts four times a year. Eventually, they took over the work of the hundred courts and the sheriffs' courts.

- In 1285, Edward I passed a new law declaring that men had a duty to help form a *posse comitatus* (force of the county) to help the sheriff to chase and catch criminals. This was an extension of the traditional tithings' practice of hue and cry.

Activities

3 How does the work of Henry II illustrate the importance of a strong monarch in providing law and order?

Summary

- A system of common law was developed in the reign of Henry II, which is the basis of the legal system today.
- The Church also remained a powerful legal force and kept its own courts.

4.11 Crime and punishment in the later Middle Ages

Learning outcomes

By the end of this topic you should be able to:

- describe what kinds of crimes were committed during the later Middle Ages
- explain why there were still challenges to authority at this time.

Challenges to royal authority

Despite the reforms made under Henry II and some of his successors, the system of justice still depended to a great extent on the character and abilities of the king. If a king was either not interested in law and order or was just weak, the rule of law and the king's peace soon began to break down. This happened under Edward II and Henry VI. Problems also arose sometimes when strong and active kings were absent because of war – for instance, at times during the reigns of Richard I, Edward I and Edward III.

During the 14th and 15th centuries in particular, some rich and powerful families ('overmighty subjects') felt strong enough to ignore the law and the king himself. There was also a lengthy period of disruption and civil war in the later 15th century known as the Wars of the Roses. Crime and disorder increased in the country during this civil war.

Religion and crime

Another crime and another form of rebellion against authority which occurred in the later Middle Ages (and which was harshly punished) was that of heresy. Church leaders saw any views that differed from the official Roman Catholic teachings as a serious challenge to their authority. The government supported them in this. Consequently, the Church's special courts could have such people arrested and tortured and, if found guilty, they could be executed. In the early 15th century, John Wyclif and his followers, who were known as the Lollards, posed the largest challenge to the Roman Catholic Church in England.

Source A: Extracts from the Act of 1401, 'On the Burning of Heretics'.

'Many false persons do maliciously preach and teach these new doctrines [those of Wyclif and the Lollards] against the holy Catholic Church; they make and write books, they wickedly instruct the people and stir them to rebellion... From henceforth... no one... shall preach openly without a licence from a bishop; no one shall make, write or possess a book of such wicked doctrines. And if any persons be convicted of acting against this law, they shall be burnt before the people in a public place...'

Activities

1 What does Source A tell us about the connection between religion and crime in the later Middle Ages? Use the source and the information on these pages to explain your answer.

2 In what ways did 'over-mighty' subjects increase crime during the later Middle Ages? Why were they able to behave in such ways?

Types of crime in the later Middle Ages

The most common types of crime remained petty or small-scale theft. Such types of crime can often be linked to poverty. Records show that at times of economic distress, the numbers of such cases often increased significantly. At the same time, the Forest Laws introduced by William I continued to cause resentment. Partly as a result of such factors, some people became outlaws. It was against such a background that stories about an outlaw called Robin Hood began to emerge in the late 14th century. Most outlaws in the Middle Ages, though, robbed the poor rather than the rich, stealing their food, clothing, animals and tools.

Source B: A pie chart showing the types of crimes committed in eight English counties in the period 1300–1348.

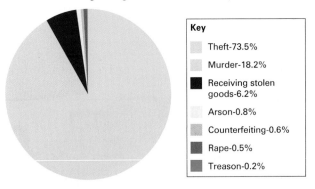

Key
- Theft-73.5%
- Murder-18.2%
- Receiving stolen goods-6.2%
- Arson-0.8%
- Counterfeiting-0.6%
- Rape-0.5%
- Treason-0.2%

Source C: A bar chart showing the different types of theft committed in Norfolk during the period 1300–1348, taken from *Crime and Punishment Through Time*, by John Murray, 1999. Thefts were usually committed by people who knew their victims and were less common in winter, when animals had been slaughtered and most goods were locked away.

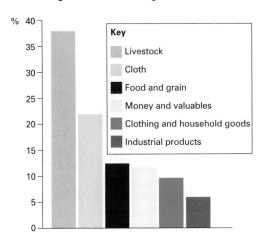

Key
- Livestock
- Cloth
- Food and grain
- Money and valuables
- Clothing and household goods
- Industrial products

Source D: A graph showing the number of criminal cases heard in the royal courts, and the price of wheat in Norfolk in the period 1300–1348, taken from *Crime and Punishment Through Time* by John Murray, 1999.

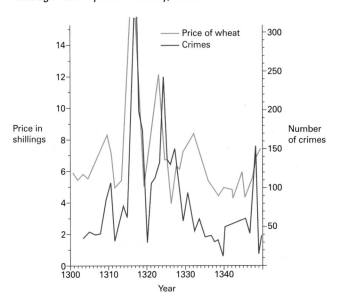

Punishment in the later Middle Ages

To begin with, executions and other physical punishments continued to be the most common types of punishment. However, as the Middle Ages continued, hanging was used less and less. In part, this was due to the influence of the Church. Many people accused of a crime were often only fined, or even pardoned. Between 1446 and 1448, 172 people received pardons from the king's court in cases ranging from theft, burglary, assault, kidnapping, and even rape and murder.

At the same time, judges frequently criticised juries for not convicting their neighbours. Often, it was only those who were accused of, or who had committed, crime on a fairly regular basis (habitual offenders) who were found guilty and punished.

Activities

3 What do Sources B and C tell us about crime in the later Middle Ages? Was this different from or similar to crime in Roman, Anglo-Saxon and Norman times?

4 Look at the patterns of criminal activity shown in Source D, opposite. What can you learn from the source?

5 Were the types of crime committed and the punishments given in the later Middle Ages any different from those in the 11th and 12th centuries?

Summary

- The power of the king was important in law enforcement.
- There were times in the later Middle Ages when crimes of rebellion and heresy increased.
- Punishments at the time were more lenient than before and many people received pardons.

Summary: Crime and punishment from Roman Britain to c1450

74

 **ROMAN PERIOD**

c50

 c50 The Romans invade and conquer

- Evidence given in court
- Decisions by magistrates

- Brutal
- Frequent use of capital punishment
- Different for orders

- Centralised
- Uniform throughout the Empire
- No police force

- Power to make laws
- Organisation to enforce them throughout the Empire

c400 The Roman army leaves Britain

 **c450 SAXON PERIOD**

 **NORMAN AND MEDIEVAL PERIOD**

c1000

- Little use of power to make laws
- Enforced the king's peace

- Not centralised
- Community responsibility
- No police force

- Less harsh than Roman
- Wirgild and botgild
- Influenced by the Church

- Oath-taking in court
- Decision by community
- Trial by ordeal if community unable to agree

 871 The beginning of the reign of Alfred the Great, King of Wessex

633 The Synod of Whitby establishes the authority of the Roman Catholic Church in Britain

1361 The justice of the Peace Act

1066 The Norman Conquest

 **1166 The Assize of Clarendon**

 **1215 The Catholic Church condemns trial by ordeal**

- Oath-taking in court
- Decision by community
- Trial by ordeal or battle if community unable to agree
- Use of juries after trial by ordeal ended

- More harsh than Anglo-Saxon
- Much corporal and capital punishment
- Became less severe, influenced by the Church

- Became more centralised during the period
- Church Courts
- Community responsibility
- No police force

 c1450
- More authority than Anglo-Saxon kings
- Power varied with strength of character
- Enforced the king's peace
- Power of law enforcement increased in the reign of Henry II

Key The role of the monarch Systems for law enforcement Methods of deciding guilt or innocence Approaches to punishment

Patterns of change

The diagram below shows changes in the community's role in law enforcement.

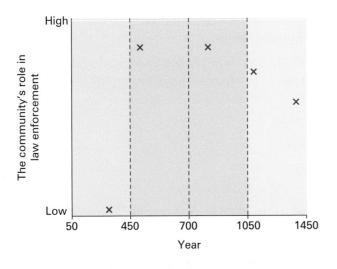

Factors causing change

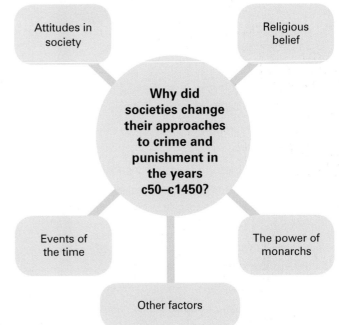

Activities

1 Draw your own graph like the one above to show patterns of change in punishment from Roman times to 1450. Place the x high when you think punishments were most harsh and lower in periods when they were less harsh.

2 Make your own graph to show the pattern of change in the roles of the monarch and of the Church in making and enforcing laws from the 1st century to the 15th century. Place the x highest when their power is highest. Put the monarch in red and the Church in green.

3 Look at your four graphs. Are there any links between the patterns? For example, are there any links between the power of the Church and the pattern in punishments?

Activities

4 How did the events of the Norman Conquest change crime and punishment in England?

5 Study the diagram above. For your three periods of study – Roman, Anglo-Saxon or medieval England – choose three factors that were important in changing the way the law was enforced. In each case decide which one you think was most important.

6 Study the road map on page 74 and the diagrams you have made. Which of the three periods is the odd one out? Explain your choice.

Could each of them be seen as the 'odd one out'? Explain your answer.

Quick quiz

1 In which century did the Roman army withdraw from Britain?

2 What important religious meeting took place in the north of England in 663 CE?

3 What, in Anglo-Saxon law, was the 'wergeld'?

4 What other method – apart from trial by jury – did the Anglo-Saxons use to decide whether someone was innocent or guilty?

5 What new set of laws was introduced by the Normans after 1066?

6 Name one way the Church was involved in criminal cases under the Normans.

7 Which king issued the Constitutions of Clarendon in 1164, in an attempt to bring together all laws and legal procedures?

8 Name the officials who, after an act of 1361, were used to help run the local justice system.

9 What did the Church stop doing in 1215 with regard to trials?

10 What new attitude to punishment did the Church try to apply to the role of punishments in the Middle Ages?

Support activity

1 Divide into groups of four to six, each group taking ONE of the four main periods covered in this unit: Roman, Anglo-Saxon, Norman and Medieval.

For whichever period you've selected, take some A3 paper and try to produce an information poster (e.g. by using spider diagrams) that deals with the following four aspects:

• types of crime

• law enforcement

• types of punishments

• attitudes to crime and punishment.

To do this as fully as possible, go over the information in this unit and any other extra information you've found to complete your poster.

When every group has completed its poster, display them in chronological order so that everyone can check to see what remained the same and what changed.

Then, individually, use these posters to:

Make your own list of *changes* and *similarities* for the three 'turning points':

• the changeover from Roman to Anglo-Saxon law

• the changeover from Anglo-Saxon to Norman law

• the changeover from Norman to later Medieval law.

2 As a final task, try explaining what caused any changes – e.g. particular problems (civil war, 'over-mighty subjects', changing attitudes).

Find out more

For more information about the subjects covered in this section, go to www.heinemann.co.uk/hotlinks (express code 4417P) and click on the appropriate link.

• The BBC website

• The History Learning site

• Spartacus School website

• The Learning curve website

Checklist

Read through the following list and evaluate how well you know and understand each of the topics.

- The types of crimes most common in the Roman, Anglo-Saxon, Norman and Medieval periods.
- Whether there were any changes during these periods concerning the most common types of crimes.
- Which sorts of crimes were considered the most serious during these different periods.
- How law enforcement changed in the period before 1066, and how it changed after that date.
- The changing role played by religion and the Church in the law and legal procedures.
- How Henry II tried to restore royal authority and law enforcement during his reign.
- What changes with regard to punishments were introduced after the Anglo-Saxons settled in Britain.
- How punishments stayed the same and how they changed after 1066.
- What important changes and problems concerning law enforcement took place in the later Middle Ages.
- How attitudes to crime and punishment changed during these periods, and the main reasons for any changes.

Introduction to the exam

This section gives you examples of the two types of question you will have to answer in this part of your exam. Remember that BOTH the (a) and (b) parts have to be answered. For part (a) you have to recall and use the main facts to describe or explain an aspect of your course; part (b) requires you to recall and evaluate information about an aspect of your course to answer a question about change or the reasons for it. Question (a) is worth 9 marks and question (b) is worth 16 marks, so allocate your time accordingly.

This section gives you student answers and examiner comments to help you understand what you need to do in such questions to get top marks.

Mini exam paper

1 Describe the key features of trial by ordeal.

(9 marks)

2 How much did the methods of trial and punishment change from the Norman period (11th century) to the early Tudor period? Explain your answer. (16 marks)

You may use the following information in your answer and any other information of your own.

- Criminals could claim sanctuary.
- Anyone who claimed Benefit of Clergy was tried by the Church Courts.
- Quarter Sessions began in 1361, where JPs would meet to deal with local crimes.

Describe the key features of trial by ordeal. (9 marks)

Student answer

The main feature of trial by ordeal was to decide if someone was guilty. There was ordeal by hot water or by hot iron. Men usually did the hot water ordeal. They had to plunge their hand or arm into boiling water to pull out an object. They were then bandaged up for three days – if the injuries stayed clean, it was a sign of innocence; if there was festering, it was taken as a sign of guilt. The hot iron ordeal was usually done by women. They had to carry a piece of hot metal for about three metres. The hands, or feet, were then bandaged for three days – the state of the wounds decided innocence or guilt.

Examiner comments

This answer gives relevant and accurate own knowledge but really only describes what happened in the ordeal. The answer needs more range. Other key features, in addition to the methods used, could include the beliefs it was based upon, and the important role played by the Church. The student has said nothing about the belief that God would make a judgement about someone's innocence or guilt, or the part played by priests. These aspects would need to be covered in order to reach the top level and so gain full marks.

Extract from an improved student answer

The main feature of trial by ordeal was to decide if someone was innocent or guilty of a crime. This method was used when the normal method of deciding guilt – where the community organised a trial, with a jury of local people who knew the accused – failed to agree a verdict.

When this happened, the Church played the leading role, as trial by ordeal was based on the belief that God would reveal his judgement about whether or not the accused had committed the crime.

The most common forms of ordeal were those by hot water (which was usually done by men), where the accused had to pull out an object…

How much did the methods of trial and punishment change from the Norman period (11th century) to the end of the Middle Ages? Explain your answer. (16 marks)

You may use the following information in your answer and any other information of your own.

- Criminals could claim sanctuary.
- Anyone who claimed Benefit of Clergy was tried by the Church courts.
- Quarter Sessions began in 1361, where JPs would meet to deal with local crimes.

Extract from a student answer

In many ways, methods of trial and punishment remained the same. After 1066, trials to decide guilt continued to operate in the same ways. The Normans continued to use local courts, although the shires were re-named as counties, and the hundred courts became manor courts. In fact, for a long time, Anglo-Saxon and Norman law ran side by side. Juries of local people continued to be used to decide a person's guilt. Also, if juries could not agree, trial by ordeal was still used by the Normans. However, one change was that the Normans introduced a new system of trial by ordeal – ordeal by combat.

However, important changes began to take place under Henry II. In 1164, he issued the Constitutions of Clarendon. From around 1200, trial by ordeal was abandoned. Instead, the system of courts and juries was strengthened and increased. In 1361, an important change was the introduction of justices of the peace. These met four times a year in new courts known as quarter sessions courts to hear criminal cases and other local issues. These took over the cases previously tried in the hundred courts. In 1461, they took over the shire or county courts from the sheriffs.

Examiner comments

This answer gives some information that is not relevant. The question begins in 1066 'from the Norman period'. The answer has some precise own knowledge about changes concerning trials and is thus clearly focused on one part of the question – i.e. the student is doing more than just describing how trials were conducted. Instead, it tries to provide explicit points about continuity and change, but the continuities are with the Anglo-Saxon periods.

To push this up to the top level and so gain full marks, an answer would need to assess how much change there was – picking up on continuities as well as changes – in the period from 1066 onwards.

The answer should also comment on some other aspects.

The bullet points are a hint to think about the role of Church courts.

Also needed are comments on the changing role of the king in trials and something on how punishments changed or stayed the same – this half of the question has been completely ignored.

Extract from an improved student answer

Between 1066 and 1485, there was a mixture of continuity and change with regard to both trials and punishment. After 1066, the Normans relied on a system of local courts – county courts and manor courts – to decide on questions of guilt or innocence. At first the system of trial by ordeal was also used. These methods of trial continued mostly unchanged for the next 100–150 years, until the Church condemned trial by ordeal. But kings also had a growing role in the justice system. Henry II set up a new royal court, the Court of King's Bench, and new travelling justices in Eyre to enforce royal justice.

Punishments in the early Norman period were often harsh – not just whippings and mutilations, but also hanging for a range of offences, including theft and arson. These were done in public to deter others. However, this began to change, mainly as a result of the growing influence of the Church, which tried to enforce the idea that punishment should be used to reform the guilty. During the later Middle Ages, hanging was used less and less. The role of the Church continued to increase, even though Henry II tried to limit its powers.

5.1 Changing views of the nature of criminal activity c1450 to present day: introduction

Introduction

In this section, you will explore three case studies of different activities that have been punished by the authorities:

- witchcraft in the 16th and 17th centuries
- conscientious objection in the 20th century
- domestic violence in the 20th century.

Aims and outcomes

You will examine the reasons for change in the way criminal activity is viewed by society. You will explore:

- why societies see certain activities as crimes in some periods and not in others
- what influences the way ordinary people see crimes
- what influences how governments act to define crimes.

Source A: An extract from *Demonologie*, written by James I in 1597.

There are so many at this time and in this country of these detestable slaves of the Devil, the witches, that it has encouraged me to write this book... so I can convince the doubting hearts of many, both that such assaults by Satan are practised and that the guilty should be punished.

Source B: An engraving from a pamphlet, showing the public hanging of three witches in Chelmsford, Essex, in 1589. Along with the three women (Joan Prentice, Joan Cony and Joan Upney), their 'familiars' can be seen. Familiars were small animals that people thought helped witches to perform their magic.

Timeline

1542	1563	1597	1604	1642–1649
Henry VIII makes witchcraft a capital offence	A law is passed that differentiates between minor and major witchcraft	*Demonologie* written by the future James I	James I brings all witchcraft laws together	Increased hysteria about witches during the English Civil War

Witchcraft

This drawing shows a method (often unofficial) of helping to decide if someone, usually a woman, was a witch. They would be 'swum' or 'floated' in a river or pond that had been blessed by a priest to make the water 'holy', to 'prove' whether or not she was a witch. If she sank, she was innocent but if she floated, it was taken as a sign of guilt, and she would then be questioned further and, if found guilty, hanged. What do beliefs and actions like this indicate? Are such beliefs entirely a thing of the past?

Domestic violence

Erin Pizzey, the founder of the first refuge for battered women in Britain. As the photograph shows, children are also deeply affected by domestic violence. Is domestic violence still a problem or has it been ended? Is it always a case of a man being violent to a woman?

Conscientious objection

This is a photograph of members of the Non-Combatant Corps who had refused to fight during the First World War, building a military road in East Anglia in 1916. Such conscientious objectors to war often received rough treatment. Do you think a refusal to fight in a war is ever justified? Would you be prepared to make such a stand?

Activities

Get in to groups of four or five. Look at Source A and the hanging of three witches in 1589 shown in Source B. Then take 5–10 minutes to discuss the following questions:

1 What beliefs do you think were necessary for people to take such actions?

2 Do you think that all such beliefs have now vanished? Try to provide evidence/ arguments to back up your views.

Share your group's ideas with your class.

1684	1916	1960	1991	1996
Last execution in England for witchcraft	First introduction of compulsory conscription in Britain during the First World War	End of National Service	Rape within marriage made a criminal offence for the first time in England and Wales	Family Law Act

5.2 Witchcraft: definitions, beliefs and laws

Learning outcomes

By the end of this topic you should be able to:

● explain what was meant by 'witchcraft'

● describe the views that people in the 16th and 17th centuries had about witches.

Before...

In the Middle Ages, people had been tried for witchcraft in Church courts, which had tended to give relatively light sentences. This was because ordinary people, who were too poor to afford the services of doctors, relied on local 'wise women'. These women, using a combination of herbal treatments and magic charms, tried to cure illnesses of both humans and animals.

Throughout the 16th and 17th centuries, many superstitions continued to survive, especially in remote rural areas, where old religions and magical beliefs from pre-Christian times continued to linger. Many people believed that a witch met with the Devil to receive instructions about what evil to commit, and that witches had animals, sent by the Devil, that were their familiars and helped them in their evil work.

Source A: A woodcut of 1579, showing an elderly witch feeding her satanic 'familiars'.

A crime created by the monarchs?

In 1542 Henry VIII passed a new law that made 'witchcraft' a serious crime in England which carried the death penalty. However, witchcraft persecutions did not really begin until the 1563 law was passed under Elizabeth I. This defined two types of witchcraft crime:

● Major witchcraft – trying to bring about a death or raise the spirits of the dead. This was punishable by death.

● Minor witchcraft – when someone used magic and charms. This was punishable by imprisonment or the stocks.

Source B: A map showing the main areas of witch-hunts in Britain in the period 1450–1750. Note that the areas with the heaviest persecutions were in East Anglia and Scotland. Protestantism was strongest in these areas.

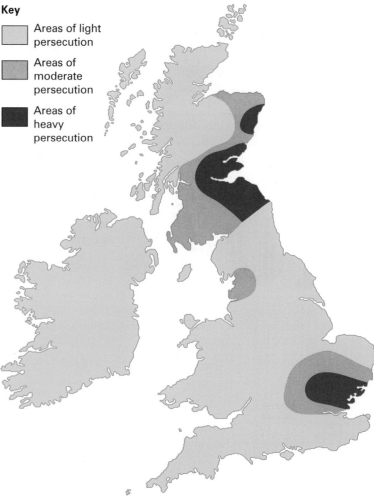

Key

Areas of light persecution

Areas of moderate persecution

Areas of heavy persecution

Witch-hunts in England did not become really significant until after the 1604 law, passed under James I, that enforced all other witchcraft laws. James believed in, and feared, witches and had written a book on it in 1597, entitled *Demonologie*. Like the Tudors before him, he also disliked the secrecy surrounding what was believed to be the practice of witchcraft. He saw this as giving opportunities for conspirators and traitors to get together. There were many plots and rebellions during this period.

Activities

1 What can you learn from Source B about witch-hunts in Britain?

Why were these new laws passed?

A combination of factors explain why witchcraft was made into such a serious crime in this period and why so many people were punished by the new laws made.

Religion

England (like much of Europe) was deeply affected by the Protestant Reformation, which challenged the control of the Roman Catholic Church. Before Henry VIII's break with Rome (see Section 1.4, pages 10–11), witchcraft had been seen as an offence against the Church. Now it was perceived as an offence against the state and its ruler. During the period 1500–1700, both Catholic and Protestant rulers and Church leaders called for action against suspected witches, calling their religious opponents 'Antichrist' as well as heretics.

Economic hardship

The period 1580–1645 saw peasants and craftsmen suffer increasing hardship as real wages and work opportunities declined, and the gap between rich and poor widened during this period, particularly in villages and small towns. The number of beggars and vagabonds increased. These economic problems sometimes led to bad feelings between neighbours. Bad luck (such as crop failures or the death of stock animals) was also blamed on evil spirits and the spells of witches, especially if someone was envious of another's success or relative prosperity. Most accusations of witchcraft, however, were made by wealthy people against poor people.

Social changes

Economic hardship led to families and small communities breaking up as some members began to move away in search of work. Many old women, previously supported by their families, found themselves on their own. In such circumstances, many turned to magic and charms as a way of trying to improve their luck and earn a living.

Civil war

Tensions in many communities were also heightened by civil wars in the years 1642–49. Significantly, once these religious and political conflicts had died down, the witchcraft craze subsided almost as quickly as it had arisen.

Activities

2 In small groups, list the causes of the increase in witch trials in Britain in the period 1500–1700 in order of importance. Then present a case for the one you think was the *main* cause. Remember to support your views with evidence.

Summary

- Henry VIII made witchcraft a capital crime in 1542.
- This was triggered by a combination of factors, such as religion and economic hardship, that led to an increasing number of prosecutions and witch-hunts until after the Civil War, 1642–49.

5.3 Discovering witchcraft

Learning outcomes

By the end of this topic you should be able to:

- describe how accusations of witchcraft were made
- explain how those found guilty of witchcraft were punished.

Why women?

In many ways, the laws against witchcraft were just another example of the unequal treatment women suffered during this period. Over 90 per cent of people accused of witchcraft between 1450 and 1750 were women. This was despite the fact that people believed that both men (warlocks) and women (witches) could practise witchcraft and black magic. The women accused usually lived alone and were old (most were over 50), as they would be more likely to know about the 'old religion'. So, why were women targeted?

- According to some historians, many men either feared or even hated women. This hatred is known as misogyny. This has led some historians to use the phrase 'gendercide' to describe the European witch-hunts.
- Christianity had always portrayed women as morally weaker than men (e.g. the story of Adam and Eve) and therefore more likely to be persuaded to do the Devil's work.
- The Puritans in particular tended to see women as temptresses, and objected to the fact that some older women carried out abortions, which was also a capital offence.

Source A: Some comments made by William Perkins, writing in the 1690s, about the 'reasons' for women's greater involvement in witchcraft.

'Woman being the weaker sex is sooner entangled by the devil's illusions with this damnable art than the man… in all ages it is found true by experience that the devil hath more easily and oftener prevailed with women than with men.'

Activities

1 Why did many people during this period think that women were more likely to be involved in witchcraft than men?

What evidence was used to convict witches?

Let's take a closer look at one of the first major witch trials – that of Agnes Waterhouse in Chelmsford, Essex, in 1565.

Source B: An account of the trial of Agnes Waterhouse written soon after it had ended.

'A twelve-year-old girl, Agnes Brown, told how she had been churning butter when a dog with a face like an ape came in with a knife between its teeth. It said it was going to kill her. When she asked who its mistress was, the animal wagged its head towards Mother Waterhouse's house.

At this, Mother Waterhouse asked what the knife was like. Agnes Brown said it was a dagger, and Mother Waterhouse says she was lying because there was no dagger in her house.'

Source C: An extract from the statement of Agnes Waterhouse at her trial. Agnes was found guilty. According to official records she was the first person to be hanged for witchcraft in England in the 16th century.

'Then said the judge: 'Agnes Waterhouse, when did your cat suck your blood?' 'Never' said she. 'No', said he, 'Let me see'. And then the gaoler lifted her scarf from her head and there were various spots on her face and one on her nose. Then said the judge 'In good faith, Agnes, when did he suck of thy blood last?' 'By my faith, good lord,' said she 'not for a fortnight'.'

Activities

2 What types of evidence were used to convict Agnes Waterhouse?

3 What can you learn from Sources B and C about the problems of witchcraft trials?

Historical records (such as Sources B and C) show a variety of evidence used to convict people of witchcraft. These included:

- Unusual marks on the woman's body, for example having an extra nipple (used to feed their 'familiars'!).
- The needle test, which was known as 'pricking'. This was done to locate the devil's mark on the witch's body (it was believed that wherever the devil touched a person, the area would be insensitive to pain).
- Neighbours could also provide evidence, for instance, if two of them had heard the accused talking to her 'familiars' or making a pact with the devil.
- The use of 'possessed' children who acted as accusers.
- Confessions (sometimes women confessed after they had been deprived of sleep for long periods of time).
- 'Proof' of guilt: if two 'proven' witches would swear that the accused was one too.
- Finally, there was also the 'swimming test', based on the medieval practice of trial by ordeal and first introduced officially into witchcraft trials in 1612 under James I.

Source D: A 17th-century woodcut from a pamphlet showing Mother Sutton undergoing the 'swimming test' after she was accused of witchcraft.

Summary

- Many more women than men were prosecuted under witchcraft laws.
- A variety of evidence was used against them.

5.4 Witch-hunts and punishments

Punishment of witches

If found guilty of major witchcraft by the courts and sentenced to death, by far the most common form of execution for witches was death by hanging. Historians have made various estimates of the number of people hanged for witchcraft in England during the period 1542–1736, when witchcraft laws were in force. Some put the number as low as 400, while many believe the probable number is around 1,000. It is difficult to arrive at a definite figure, as in remote areas there is evidence that local communities at times took the law into their own hands and applied the 'swimming test', based on the traditional method of ordeal by cold water. There are, though, no records of these unofficial 'trials'.

Source A: A chart showing accusations of witchcraft in the courts of five English counties, and the numbers executed for witchcraft in the period 1560–1700.

County	Number of accusations 1560–1700	Number of executions 1560–1700
Sussex	33	1
Surrey	71	5
Hertfordshire	81	8
Kent	132	16
Essex	473	82
Total	790	112

Witch-hunts and the Witchfinder General

Although people were accused of, and tried for, witchcraft throughout this period, there were certain times when whole communities seemed gripped by mass hysteria; for instance, during times of religious change in the middle of the 16th century under Mary I and Elizabeth I. However, mass executions of witches were very rare in England compared to some other parts of Europe (including Scotland) during the same period. For instance, in Como in North Italy, over 1,000 witches were burnt at the stake in one year.

Possibly the worst phase of witch-hunt hysteria in England took place in East Anglia during the English Civil Wars (1642–49). At this time there were conflicts over religion, and the control of the authorities was weakened by civil war. Matthew Hopkins helped to create a great panic over witches. Hopkins began his interest in witchcraft as a lawyer in Manningtree in Essex. He accused 36 women of being witches and was able to get 19 of them hanged; another nine died while they were in gaol. He and his team of 'investigators' were responsible for many deaths, and Hopkins became known as 'The Witchfinder General'. For each witch 'discovered' and then executed, Hopkins received a fee. In Essex alone in 1645, there were 36 witch trials. By 1646, Hopkins's activities were stopped. This was partly because he broke the law and used torture to gain confessions but also because, as the first Civil War came to a close, the authorities were able to reassert control over local areas.

Source B: An illustration from a book by Matthew Hopkins, called *The Discovery of Witches*.

- The reign of Charles II from 1660 saw the creation of the Royal Society and a huge increase in scientific experiments and discoveries, which were encouraged by the king. Many things that had been seen as the work of evil spirits and spells began to be explained by science.

Despite these changing attitudes, the last execution in England for witchcraft was of Alice Molland in Exeter in 1684 and witchcraft continued to be a crime until all laws concerning witchcraft were abolished in 1736.

Most uneducated people (especially in remote rural areas) still clung to their belief in the old superstitions and the supernatural. For instance, in 1751, in Tring, Hertfordshire, Ruth Osborne was accused of witchcraft by her neighbours and was unofficially subjected to the swimming test. She died as a result of the test; later, though, one of the main ringleaders was hanged for her murder. This illustrates that the attitudes of the authorities had clearly changed, even if local beliefs had not.

Activities

3 Construct a spider diagram to show the various reasons for the decline in witch-hunting. Then write a short paragraph to explain what you think was the most important reason.

4 Copy graph (a) on page 99, which shows the pattern of changes in the number of prosecutions for witchcraft. Beside it make a similar graph to show the pattern of changes in the attitudes of the authorities and attitudes of the general public to witches. Place the 'x' higher when the fear is greater. Put the authorities in red and the public in green.

Activities

1 Find three reasons why witchcraft hysteria occurred in the 16th and 17th centuries.

2 Think about the role of the authorities. How did they play a part in each of the reasons you have found?

Why did witchcraft trials decline?

After the end of the Civil Wars the number of people accused of witchcraft declined for various reasons.

- Economic and social change began to slow down, as many people started to become better off and share in the prosperity. This reduced the tensions in villages and so most people became less jealous and suspicious of their neighbours.
- Although many people still believed in witches and the devil, in general, a growing number of people were taking a more rational attitude to what they now saw as superstitions.

Summary

- Although they were far less extensive than in other parts of Europe, there were periods of witch-hunts in England where many people were brought to trial.
- Up to 1,000 people were executed as witches.
- By the mid-17th century the number of these trials began to decline as superstitious beliefs were being replaced by scientific explanations.

5.5 What is conscientious objection?

Learning outcomes

By the end of this topic you should be able to:

- describe what conscientious objection is
- explain why this sometimes became a crime during the 20th century.

Before...

In wars before the 20th century, professional armies, mostly made up of volunteers, had done the fighting. This meant that no one who was opposed to war was forced to fight. Anyone objecting to war simply avoided joining up.

What is conscientious objection?

Conscientious objectors are people who have religious, moral or political objections either to all wars or, less commonly, to a particular war.

Religious

Some religious groups, most famously the Quakers, are opposed to all war. Such Christian groups point out that the Ten Commandments in the Bible includes the phrase 'Thou shalt not kill', and that Jesus Christ advised his followers to 'turn the other cheek' when attacked.

Moral

People who believe that all war is morally wrong are called Pacifists. They believe that war never solves problems but, in fact, creates new ones leading to yet another war.

Political

There are also people who object to particular wars for political reasons; for instance, many socialists and communists see most wars as being fought to protect or increase the wealth of big companies, so they refuse to fight in such wars.

Source A: An extract from a statement issued by the Independent Labour Party (ILP) when war was declared in August 1914.

'Out of the darkness we hail our working-class comrades of every land. Across the roar of guns we send sympathy and greetings to the German Socialists. They are no enemies of ours, but faithful friends.'

Activities

1 Explain the three main objections to war held by conscientious objectors.

2 What kind of conscientious objectors do you think the writers of Source A belonged to? Give reasons for your answer.

Why did conscientious objectors become a problem?

Opposition to war became a serious political and criminal issue in Britain in the 20th century with the introduction of conscription (compulsory military service) for both the First and Second World Wars.

Both of these wars were 'total' wars. They were so big that the government felt it necessary to involve the whole of society in the war effort. This meant that the state introduced a new law which said that everyone within a certain age group who was fit and healthy and not working in a job that was essential to running the country such as farming or mining, was legally obliged to fight in one of the armed forces.

Conscription was first introduced in 1916 as, after three years of total war, there were not enough people choosing to join the army, navy or air force. Unlike some other European countries, when the First World War ended so did conscription in Britain, but once the Second World War began in

September 1939, conscription soon followed in October. That meant that during these periods of conscription, people who refused to fight were breaking the law and could therefore be punished.

Source B: A poster issued after the introduction of conscription in 1916. It advises people that unless they get an exemption certificate, they will have to join the armed forces.

MILITARY SERVICE ACT, 1916

Every man to whom the Act applies will on Thursday, March 2nd, be deemed to have enlisted for the period of the War unless he is excepted or exempt.

Any man who has adequate grounds for applying to a Local Tribunal for a

CERTIFICATE OF EXEMPTION UNDER THIS ACT

Must do so BEFORE

THURSDAY, MARCH 2

Why wait for the Act to apply to you?

Come _now_ and join of your own free will.

You can _at once put your claim_ before a Local Tribunal _for exemption_ from being called up for Military Service if you wish.

ATTEST NOW

Published by the PARLIAMENTARY AND JOINT LABOUR RECRUITING COMMITTEES, LONDON.   POSTER No. 159.   Wt. W. 17147 783.

However, the introduction of compulsory military service raised a series of legal and moral questions. On the one hand, it can be argued that a democratically elected government passes laws for the good of the people as a whole, in which case everyone should obey the law even if they object to it. However, there is also the question of individual conscience. What if the law goes against some fundamental moral, political or religious belief held by that individual? Does that individual have the right to disregard a law that goes against their views? In particular, what if the state asks you to kill someone else by getting you to fight in a war?

People who refuse to obey such laws are known as conscientious objectors. However, as we shall see, because it was breaking the law, the refusal to fight was seen as a 'crime' and one that the authorities were determined to punish.

Activities

3 Explain how the beginning of conscription created a new crime during the first half of the 20th century.

4 Discuss in small groups whether you think conscientious objectors should be punished by the law.

5 How is this 'crime' different from the 'crime' of witchcraft? Clue: think about what caused both to be classed as crimes.

Summary

- Conscientious objectors disagree with war for religious, moral or political reasons.
- The arrival of the two world wars led the government to introduce conscription, which meant that people refusing to take part in the war could now be imprisoned.

5.6 Conscientious objection in the First World War

Learning outcomes

By the end of this topic you should be able to:

- explain how many people became conscientious objectors during the First World War
- describe what they did and how they were treated.

Attitudes of society

During the First World War, conscientious objectors, sometimes referred to as 'conchies' or 'COs', were a group of protesters who aroused particular resentment and hostility. When the war began in 1914 the army at first relied on volunteers to sign up to fight.

One significant group of people who objected to war were the Quakers (Society of Friends). They helped to organise the No-Conscription Fellowship. This fellowship tried to hold meetings and give support to those who wished to object to the war. Their meetings were often violently broken up by the police and by members of the public who, influenced by government propaganda, saw the COs as cowards or even traitors.

However, conscription (compulsory call-up) was introduced in 1916. The law, which introduced conscription, included a clause – put in at the insistence of Quaker MPs – that those who objected to military service on the grounds of conscience could be excused. Although the law accepted that people had the right to conscientious objection, men who refused military service at this time were sometimes imprisoned and often treated harshly by their community. Special 'courts' known as military tribunals were set up to see which people could be excused military service. These tribunals were made up of army officers and local middle-class people such as doctors and clergymen. About 16,000 men refused to fight in the war for reasons of conscience, although it made them very unpopular with many of the public.

The military tribunals had the power to decide whether, in their opinion, such people had 'genuine' reasons for objecting to involvement in the war. If the tribunals accepted their reasons, they were given Exemption Certificates. However, only 400 conscientious objectors were given complete exemption on the grounds of conscience.

Source A: Two of the comments made by members of military tribunals to COs.

'It is such people as you who cause wars…'

'You are only fit to be on the end of a German bayonet.'

Activities

1 Do you think Source A shows that conscientious objectors would always get a fair hearing at military tribunals?

2 Laws and punishment often reflect how people are thinking at the time.

What links can you find between people's thinking and

(i) the punishing of conscientious objectors

(ii) the punishing of witches in the 16th and 17th centuries? (See pages 82–87.)

The 'alternativists'

The majority of conscientious objectors were known as 'alternativists'. The alternativists refused to do anything to kill or injure anyone, but were prepared to take part in the war in alternative ways by doing non-combatant war work such as driving ambulances or being stretcher-bearers. Several COs won medals for bravery in carrying out their duties at the front. However, many employers refused to give jobs to such people and in the end the government had to set up its own work camps, such as quarries where COs crushed stone for use in road repairs.

Source B: Members of the Non-Combatant Corps, published in *The Illustrated War News* on 23 August 1916. These men were conscientious objectors, and are shown constructing a military road in East Anglia. Other members of the NCC were sent to work in France.

Home Work for a Rare "Bird," the Conscientious Objector.

CONSCIENTIOUS OBJECTORS USEFULLY EMPLOYED : MEN OF THE N.C.C. ON A MILITARY ROAD.

In order to utilise the services of conscientious objectors, it will be remembered, the military authorities formed a Non-Combatant Corps, to be employed on various kinds of useful work. Our photographs show some of the men employed on the construction of a military road in East Anglia. Others of the corps have been sent to France, where the first batches arrived early in May.

"At present," wrote Mr. Philip Gibbs shortly afterwards, "they are engaged on railway work ; but afterwards, if they are strong enough, they will be put to stiffer work. ' It is part of our faith,' said one of them, 'that it is wrong to take human life. If we became combatants we should deny our faith.' " Another said : "It 's not cowardice that brings us here."—[Photo. by L.N.A.]

The 'absolutists'

However, about 1,500 conscientious objectors refused to do anything to assist in a war they felt was fundamentally wrong. These 'absolutists' were treated as criminals and sent to prison – often military prisons at first. They received very harsh and often brutal treatment from the prison warders, and were usually forced to do hard labour. Some were taken to France, forced into military uniforms and threatened with execution if they did not obey military orders in a war zone. When this failed to change their minds, they were sent back to civilian prisons in Britain, or kept in military prisons in France, where punishments were often extremely brutal.

In all, ten COs died in prison and another 63 died shortly after their release. In addition, 31 had

mental breakdowns, often as a result of being put in solitary confinement. At the end of the war, all COs were denied the right to vote for five years and many found it impossible to get jobs; some were beaten up when they returned home.

Source C: Questions asked by two MPs in the House of Commons in July 1917, about the treatment experienced by war resisters in military prisons in Cleethorpes and Hornsea. James Brightmore was told by an officer that five of his companions had been sent to France and shot, and that he would be next.

'... the Under-Secretary of State for War [was asked] whether he is aware that... a conscientious objector..., James Brightmore, at Cleethorpes Camp, was kept for a prolonged period in a pit 10 feet deep and 40 inches by 18 inches wide, and full of water... ; and whether he has yet had a Report on the case of five [other] conscientious objectors, in the 3rd. Manchester Regiment... sent to France.

... the Under-Secretary of State for War [was also asked] whether he can now give information concerning the ill-treatment of a conscientious objector named Jack Gray, in the camp at Hornsea, [who] was ... put into a sack and repeatedly thrown into a pond, and pulled out by a rope round his body.'

Activities

3 Why do you think COs were treated in the way described in Source C?

4 Divide into groups of four and discuss which of the following descriptions of conscientious objectors in the First World War is the most appropriate: cowards, traitors or brave men? Remember to back your views with information.

Summary

- Conscientious objectors (around 16,000 men) were treated with great hostility by the general public during the First World War.
- Alternativists did other types of war work.
- Absolutists refused to support the war in any way. They were treated very harshly and punished by the authorities.

5.7 Conscientious objection in the Second World War

Learning outcomes

By the end of this topic you should be able to:

- explain what happened to conscientious objectors during the Second World War
- compare how their treatment had changed since the First World War.

Changing attitudes?

As the full horrors of the First World War emerged, many people turned to pacifism in the inter-war period. Such people included those who had previously won medals for bravery but who came to see war as horrifically wasteful and not the best way of solving disputes.

Therefore, when the Second World War broke out in 1939, there were many more conscientious objectors and this time they were not persecuted by the authorities in the same way. The government made more effort to give COs jobs in farming or industry, and it was rare for them to be sent to prison. As in the First World War, tribunals were set up to decide if people had legitimate reasons for refusing to be conscripted. This time, though, the tribunals were different: the military were not allowed to sit on them and the membership had to be representative of all social classes.

How many conscientious objectors were there in the Second World War?

In all, 59,192 people (including women) claimed exemption; all except 12,204 were given complete or partial exemption. Most of them were associated with the Central Board for Conscientious Objectors or the Quakers (Society of Friends) and co-operated with the authorities. About 29,000 did work in factories or on the land. However, some COs agreed to do non-combatant work in the armed forces, very often acting as ambulance drivers or doing dangerous jobs such as bomb disposal.

Source A: Members of a team of conscientious objectors serving with a Royal Engineers bomb-disposal squad during the Second World War. They are digging a hole to reach a mine found buried in the grounds of an isolation hospital at Dartford.

Many COs, though, were part of the Peace Pledge Union, which was opposed to war and which tried to encourage people not to fight. These tended to refuse to do any war-related activity, but, unlike the treatment of conscientious objectors during the First World War, the authorities were reluctant to send such people to prison.

Source B: Comments made by the Prime Minister, Neville Chamberlain, when reintroducing conscription in 1939.

'Where scruples are conscientiously held we desire that they should be respected and that there should be no persecution of those who hold them.'

Activities

1 Compare the response of the authorities to COs in the First and Second World Wars. For example, how were tribunals similar and different?

2 Do you think that conscientious objectors in the Second World War were cowards? Explain your answer.

They were even allowed to continue their campaign during the war, for instance, putting up posters to encourage people to refuse to fight.

However, while the attitudes of the authorities towards conscientious objectors had changed since the First World War, the attitudes of the general public had changed very little, and some members of the public were very hostile. Once again, COs were accused of being cowards and traitors, both to their faces and in the newspapers. Some COs were physically attacked, while others were sacked from their jobs. Generally, though, COs this time did not suffer as badly as COs had during the First World War.

Source C: An extract from a book about Britain during the Second World War, published in 1969.

'Six Peace Pledge Union organisers were on trial at Bow Street police court for putting up a poster which said 'War will cease when men refuse to fight. What are YOU doing about it?'. The magistrate dismissed the case, saying 'This is a free country. We are fighting to keep it a free country, as I understand it'.'

ResultsPlus
Build better answers

How much did attitudes to conscientious objectors change in the years 1916–45? (16 marks)

 Basic, Level 1 (1–4 marks)
These answers usually make general comments without detail. For example, 'People still called them cowards'.

 Good, Level 2 (5–8 marks)
Good answers provide more detail, for example, about ways in which COs were still persecuted.

 Better, Level 3 (9–12 marks)
Level 3 answers make comparisons to show the similarity or difference with the First World War, for example, in the way the authorities dealt with COs.

Excellent, Level 4 (13–16 marks)
These also weigh up the amount of change, for example, showing how much the attitudes of the authorities and the general public had changed, and that they had not changed to the same extent.

Activities

3 How far do Sources B and C show that attitudes towards conscientious objectors had changed considerably since the First World War? Why do you think this change happened?

4 Copy graph (b) on page 99, which shows changes in the pattern of prosecutions for conscientious objection. Beside it, make a similar graph to show the pattern of changes in the attitudes of the authorities to COs and changes in the attitudes of the general public. Put the authorities in red and the public in green. Put the x higher when there is more hostility to COs.

5 During the Second World War the authorities were more understanding and tolerant of COs than many of the general public. Can you see any similarities with the patterns of attitudes in the late 17th century towards the crime of witchcraft?

After...

Since 1960 (when conscription ended), Britain has had a professional volunteer army, but the question of conscientious objection has not gone away entirely. For instance, in 2003 during the Iraq War, two British soldiers were sent home from the front after expressing concerns to their fellow soldiers and their officer that they were being asked to fight an illegal war, and that they might therefore be called to account for the deaths of innocent civilians.

Summary

- There were more conscientious objectors in the Second World War than there were in the First World War.

- During the Second World War the authorities treated conscientious objectors more sympathetically and far fewer were punished as 'criminals', although they were still persecuted by the general public.

5.8 Domestic violence before 1970

Before...

During the 19th century, some women had campaigned for equal legal rights for women and had achieved some success with regard to divorce, child custody, education and property ownership, but little had been done about domestic violence.

What is domestic violence?

Domestic violence is generally understood to be the physical abuse of a wife or female partner by the husband or male partner. Hence the use of such terms as 'battered wife' or 'wife beating'. However, many today would argue that this definition is too narrow, as it takes no account of verbal bullying, mental abuse, abuse within gay or lesbian relation-ships, or domestic violence against men by women.

Women and the common law

Before the 20th century, it was generally accepted, both by the law and by many people, that husbands (and fathers) had a right to beat their wives and children. British common law once stated that it was legal for a man to chastise his wife 'in moderation'. Also, until the early 19th century, a woman who killed her husband could be found guilty of the more serious crime of 'petty treason' rather than murder. In other words, the law considered that a woman who murdered her husband, even in self-defence, had committed a much more serious crime than a husband who murdered his wife.

It was generally believed that there was a 'rule of thumb' about what level of violence from a husband against a wife was 'acceptable'. This relates to an alleged legal ruling of 1782 by Judge Sir Francis Buller that English law allowed a man to beat his

wife with a stick, so long as it was no thicker than his thumb. There is no evidence that he made such a ruling but, in 1783, the satirist James Gillray published a cartoon attacking Buller (Source A).

Source A:
A cartoon of 1783 by James Gillray, portraying Judge Buller as 'Judge Thumb'. The caption reads: *'Thumbsticks, for family correction: warranted lawful!'*

Activities

1 What can you learn from Source A (above) and Source B (page 95) about the law and past attitudes towards domestic violence?

Powerless and silent victims

Some women who suffered 'severe violence' from their husbands applied for a peace bond under civil law. These dated back to the 14th century and usually imposed a fine on particularly violent husbands. However, only wealthy women could afford this.

In the 19th century, laws were changed so that violence against wives was classed as criminal assault. However, judges often stuck to Common Law ideas that a husband had the right to 'moderately chastise' his wife. Occasionally, men who 'went too far' were punished, but this was usually by the local community rather than by the law. Newspapers during the 19th century did report particularly severe cases of wife beating, as seen in Source C (page 95).

Source B: A *Punch* cartoon published in 1874. This cartoon is commenting on the struggle of women for equal rights under the law. However, note the stick carried by the brutal husband. This may be a reference to the alleged 'rule of thumb' legal ruling referred to in Source A.

" WOMAN'S WRONGS."

BRUTAL HUSBAND. "AH! YOU'D BETTER GO SNIVELLIN' TO THE 'OUSE O' COMMONS, *YOU* HAD! MUCH THEY'RE LIKELY TO DO FOR YER! YAH! READ THAT!"

There are many factors that explain why the authorities were so slow to act:

- The general attitude was that the law should only apply to public life – the (male-dominated) authorities did not want to interfere in private family matters. As a result, much male violence was either ignored or even accepted in certain circumstances. Men who were convicted of 'criminal assault' against their wives received very light punishments such as a fines or short prison sentences.
- Before 1918, women had little political power. Women could not vote for Members of Parliament or be elected themselves. Issues that were important to women were not really considered by politicians of the time. All laws were made by men.

- The law was also enforced by men. The all-male police force was often reluctant to intervene in what they saw as 'domestic incidents'.
- Domestic violence was seen as part of the problem of 'drunkenness and disorder' among the working classes. Violence within middle- and upper-class households was rarely reported by the newspapers.
- Women themselves were often too scared to speak out and make complaints against their husbands.

Source C: Comments made by a magistrate in Liverpool, 1870, on the case against Patrick Doran, published in the Liverpool *Mercury*, 27 July 1870, in a report entitled: 'A COWARDLY WIFE BEATER'.

'… those fellows who [strike] women [are] those who [dare] not exercise their fists upon men. It [makes my] blood boil to hear these cases day after day of such brutes as the prisoner who [have] women in their power.'

Activities

2 What can you learn from Source B about domestic violence in the late 19th century? Explain your answer by referring closely to the source.

3 Construct a priority pyramid of reasons why the law was slow to take action on domestic violence. Explain why you have given priority to the reason you have placed at the top.

4 Witchcraft was an invented crime for which mainly women were punished. Domestic violence was an actual crime, mainly against women, which was not punished for centuries. What part do you think attitudes in society played in both these cases?

Summary

- Domestic violence is physical or verbal abuse by one partner towards the other in a relationship.
- Before the 20th century it was accepted that the male head of the family could beat his wife and children, and that this was a private 'family' matter and not one that should concern the law.

5.9 Why did domestic violence become a 'crime' after 1970?

Learning outcomes

By the end of this topic you should be able to:

- explain the developments that took place after 1970
- evaluate which factors were most important in leading to the classification of domestic violence as a 'crime'.

Forces for change

Various factors began to change attitudes towards domestic violence.

Campaign groups – The feminist ideas of the Women's Liberation Movement became a strong force in the 1960s. They created pressure for changes to women's rights.

New ideas about the role of the state – There was an increasing acceptance that the state could intervene in family life to improve the quality of life of its citizens. For example, laws in the early 20th century were passed to protect children. In the mid-20th century the National Health Service was developed to improve health care for all the family.

Power of the vote – In 1918 some women were granted the vote and in 1928 women were granted equal voting rights with men. Women's concerns became increasingly important to those trying to win the female vote and women themselves could be elected to parliament.

Media – Both broadcast and print media gave increasing coverage to domestic violence stories. More television programmes began to deal with this problem in dramas and 'soap-operas'. For instance, from 1993 to 1995, *Brookside* on Channel 4 ran a high-profile domestic violence storyline concerning the Jordache family.

Activities

1 Which change factor above do you think had the most influence on public attitudes? Why?

Campaign groups

During the late 1960s and 1970s, women's liberation groups and movements developed in Britain. They were determined to increase public awareness about the inequalities suffered by women, and change attitudes towards a problem that was often hidden away behind closed doors as a taboo subject. Women's groups held public marches and rallies. Their activities began to interest the media and were covered by newspapers, radio and television. Women's Aid groups campaigned to provide help for what became known as 'battered wives'. The first ever refuge for victims of domestic violence, Chiswick Women's Aid, was set up by Erin Pizzey in 1971. Soon, there were 40 refuges across the country.

In 1974 the National Women's Aid Federation was established as the first national organisation concerned with domestic violence in the UK. It brought together all the refuge services across the country and helped improve support for women and children who experienced domestic violence. It also increased pressure on the government to change the law.

Source A: The seventh demand of the Women's Liberation Movement, adopted at their 1978 National Conference.

> [We demand] freedom from intimidation by threat or use of violence or sexual coercion; and an end to all laws, assumptions and attitudes which perpetuate male dominance and men's aggression towards women.

Source B: Women's Aid protest march in the 1970s.

Source C: Comments made by one of the legal experts giving evidence to the Parliamentary Select Committee.

> What I don't want to see for battered wives is what we saw with battered children: the only way the law in this country will protect is when it is faced with a corpse... Certainly, women have died through this sort of attitude, and if this Committee can in some way recommend that the police prosecute, I would ask them to do so.

Voices in parliament

In 1971, the MP Jack Ashley raised the issue of domestic violence for the first time in parliament. Shortly afterwards, parliament set up the Select Committee on Violence in Marriage to look into the problem and consider whether the law should be changed.

Resistance

As well as increasing the pressure on the government for the laws to change, these different forces were also putting more pressure on the legal authorities to start to act on domestic violence. These authorities resisted this, with the Police Superintendents' Association and the Chief Police Officers' Association claiming that existing laws were sufficient for them to deal with violence in the home.

Various police and judicial representatives also argued that such violence was relatively insignificant when compared to 'more serious problems' such as theft and vehicle offences! The London Metropolitan Police were even concerned that involving the police in cases of domestic violence would place great strains on manpower and so prevent them from 'safeguarding other members of the public'.

ResultsPlus
Build better answers

What factors changed attitudes to domestic violence in the 20th century? (9 marks)

■ **Basic (1–3 marks)**
These answers usually make general comments without detail – for example, women had more rights.

● **Good (4–6 marks)**
Good answers will provide more detail – for example, describing the actions of the Women's Liberation Movement.

▲ **Excellent (7–9 marks)**
These answers will show how factors changed attitudes – for example, showing that the actions of the women's movements highlighted the problem of domestic violence and raised public awareness.

Domestic violence becomes a crime

In 1976, the Domestic Violence Act enabled victims to get two kinds of protection from the courts:

- non-molestation orders

- exclusion orders, which prohibited a violent abuser from returning to the home.

In 1991, rape within marriage was classed as a criminal offence in England and Wales for the first time (it was criminalised in Scotland in 1982).

In 1996, the Family Law Act gave extra protection to victims of violent partners and made arrest automatic in cases where violence had been used or threatened.

In 2004, the Domestic Violence, Crime and Victims Act gave all victims, male and female, the same protection. It also increased the powers of the police and the courts to act against abusers. Anyone breaking a non-molestation order could be charged with a criminal offence, punishable by up to five years in prison.

The 1976 Domestic Violence Act was a beginning, but it had weaknesses, mainly because of the attitudes of judges. The exclusion orders were rarely used as judges were reluctant to grant them unless the violence was severe. Judges were also reluctant to give police the power to arrest suspects who broke a court order, because it involved police in family matters.

So, after centuries where violence in the home went largely ignored and unpunished, the position has changed rapidly since 1976. A new crime has been defined, and punishments for domestic violence have become more severe.

It is important to note that these changes to the law apply to men as well as women, but it would be fair to say that public attitudes towards 'battered men' are very different.

Estimates suggest that over 30 per cent of domestic violence is against men but very few male victims come forward.

Activities

2 Domestic violence (DV), witchcraft and conscientious objection (CO) are crimes made by new laws. Can you see any differences between DV and the other two in the way this process of defining new crimes happened?

3 Do you think society turns a blind eye to male victims of domestic violence? If so, why?

4 Copy graph (c) on page 99, which shows changes in the pattern of prosecutions for domestic violence. Beside it, make a similar graph to show the pattern of changes in the attitudes of the authorities to domestic violence and changes in the attitudes of the general public. Put the authorities in red and the public in green. Put the x higher when there is more concern about DV.

After...

A study in 2004 found that one in four women and one in six men had been victims of domestic violence at some point in their lives.

Summary

- A combination of factors has led to changes in social attitudes towards domestic violence, which has forced changes in the law so that it is now regarded as a serious criminal offence and punished as such.

- These changes have not applied in practice so much to domestic violence against men by women.

98

Summary: Changing views of the nature of criminal activity c1450 to present day

Activities

1 Study the three summary graphs below and your own graphs that you made of the changing attitudes in the three case studies and the three summary graphs. What do they show you about:
 • Changes in what is seen as a crime.
 • Changes in the attitudes of the general public and how this can impact on what is defined as a criminal activity.
 • Changes in the attitudes of the authorities and how this can impact on what is defined as a criminal activity.

2 How did the events and circumstances of the time:
 • turn 'witchcraft' into a serious crime that carried the death penalty in the 16th and 17th centuries
 • create the 'crime' of conscientious objection in the early 20th century?

3 For your three case studies, choose four factors that were important in changing the definitions of criminal activity. In each case, decide which one you think was most important.

4 Which of the three 'crimes' is the odd one out – witchcraft, conscientious objection or domestic violence? Explain your choice.

 Could each of them be seen as the 'odd one out'?

The changing attitudes of the authorities

(a) Prosecutions for witchcraft

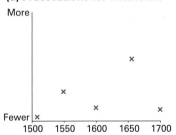

(b) Prosecutions for conscientious objection

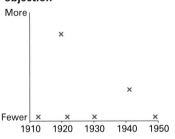

(c) Prosecutions for domestic violence

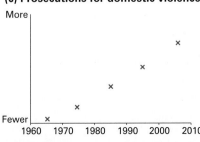

Fear

Events of the time

20th Century News
BRITAIN DECLARES WAR

Other factors

Why do societies change their definitions of criminal activity?

Public attitudes

Matthew Hopkins Witch Finder Generall

The work of organisations

The actions of governments

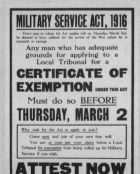

MILITARY SERVICE ACT, 1916

Any man who has adequate grounds for applying to a Local Tribunal for a

CERTIFICATE OF EXEMPTION UNDER THIS ACT

Must do so BEFORE

THURSDAY, MARCH 2

ATTEST NOW

Quick quiz

1 When did James I bring all the witchcraft laws together?

2 What was a witch's 'familiar'?

3 Who was largely responsible for a mass hysteria about witchcraft (or a 'witchcraze') in Essex and other East Anglian counties in the period 1644–47?

4 When was the last hanging of someone found guilty of witchcraft?

5 What do the initials 'CO' stand for?

6 Why did the 1916 Conscription Act cause problems for those who had moral, political or religious objections to war?

7 What were 'absolutist' COs?

8 When was the first Domestic Violence Act passed?

9 When was rape within marriage first made a criminal offence in England and Wales?

10 Which Act gave men the same protection against domestic violence as women?

Support activity

Divide into groups of four to six, each group taking ONE of the three topics covered in this unit.

For whichever topic you've selected, take some A3 paper and try to produce an information poster (e.g. by using spider diagrams) that shows why the attitudes of (a) the authorities and (b) the general public towards this crime altered during the relevant period. To do this as fully as possible, go over the information in this section and any other extra information you've found to complete your poster.

When every group has completed its poster, display them so that everyone can check to see what points they may have missed.

Then, individually, use these posters to make your own list of factors for **each** of the three topics. As a final task, you could try ranking them in order of importance.

Checklist

Read through the following list and evaluate how well you know and understand each of the topics.

- The kinds of people who were usually accused of witchcraft.
- The different reasons why accusations of witchcraft increased in the 16th and early 17th centuries.
- How witchcraft trials were usually conducted and the methods used to establish 'guilt'.
- The reasons why such trials began to decline in the period 1650–1700.
- The definition of 'conscientious objection'.
- How conscientious objectors were treated in the First World War.
- Why COs were treated more leniently during the Second World War.
- What is meant by the term 'domestic violence'.
- How attitudes to domestic violence altered during the 20th century.
- The main reasons for these changes in attitudes.

Find out more

For more information about the subjects covered in this section, go to www.heinemann.co.uk/hotlinks (express code 4417P) and click on the appropriate link.

General
- The BBC website
- The History Learning site
- Spartacus School website
- The Learning curve website

Witchcraft
- Elizabethan website
- Hulford website
- Pendle witches website
- Pendle life website
- Lancashire website
- BBC website

Conscientious objectors
- National Archives website
- PPU website
- Quakers website

Domestic violence
- Domestic violence

Introduction to the exam

In this exam you will have to answer an (a) and a (b) question on this topic. For the (a) part you have to recall and use the main facts to describe or explain an aspect of your course; the (b) part requires you to recall and evaluate information about an aspect of your course to answer a question about change or the reasons for it. Question (a) is worth 9 marks and question (b) 16 marks, so allocate your time accordingly.

Mini exam paper

1 (a) Describe the main experiences of conscientious objectors during the First World War. (9 marks)

(b) Why were conscientious objectors treated more leniently in the Second World War than they were in the First World War? (16 marks)

You may use the following in your answer and any other information of your own.

- Over 1,000 conscientious objectors were imprisoned in Dartmoor prison in 1916.
- Many conscientious objectors acted as stretcher carriers on the battlefields of the First World War.
- In the Second World War the government tried to give conscientious objectors jobs in farming and industry.

---

2 (a) Describe the changes to the law after 1970 that improved protection for victims of domestic violence. (9 marks)

(b) How important were campaign groups in getting the law on domestic violence changed? Explain your answer. (16 marks)

You may use the following in your answer and any other information of your own.

- 'Women's lib' groups campaigned in the 1960s.
- A parliamentary select committee was set up to look into the issue of domestic violence in 1974.
- Channel 4's *Brookside* series featured the issue of domestic violence in the 1990s.

Describe the main experiences of conscientious objectors during the First World War. (9 marks)

Student answer

The main experience of conscientious objectors during the First World War was of hostility; sometimes they were even beaten up. People thought that conscientious objectors were cowards and even traitors.

Military tribunals, which were special courts, were set up to see who could be excused military service. 16,000 'COs' in the First World War had their cases heard by tribunals. These tribunals could give exemption certificates if COs had genuine reasons of conscience. Most of the 16,000 were refused exemption.

The COs were then sent to prisons, such as Dartmoor. There they received very harsh treatment from the prison warders and were usually given hard labour, or were kept in solitary confinement.

Examiner comments

This answer gives some relevant and precise own knowledge.

However, the answer misses out some other important aspects of the treatment and experiences of conscientious objectors during the First World War. In fact, the prison experiences described in the answer only relate to the small minority of 'absolutist' COs. The experiences of the 'alternativists' would need to be covered also.

To push this up to the top level and so gain full marks, the student would need to comment on the alternativists, what COs did in Britain and France, and the experiences of religious COs.

Improved student answer

The main experience of the 16,000 or so COs during the First World War was generally one of hostility and even violence, as most people thought they were cowards and even traitors. However, their experiences varied, according to what type of CO they were. For instance, those objecting on religious grounds usually got more sympathetic treatment from the military tribunals which were set up to decide who could be excused military service on grounds of conscience, than those whose objections were political.

Most of the 16,000 were refused exemption; of these, most were men who refused to actually fight in the war and so injure or kill someone, but who were prepared to do non-combatant duties. Such COs – known as 'alternativists' – either did military-related or agricultural work in Britain, or worked as stretcher-bearers or ambulance drivers on the front-line: several of them won medals for bravery.

However, a small minority – known as 'absolutists' – refused to do anything that contributed to the war effort. Such COs were sent to military prisons, where the treatment was often worse. Some were taken to France, where they were forced to put on military uniforms. They were then told that they were now in a war zone and that, if they refused to obey military orders, they would be shot, although this did not happen.

Why were accusations of witchcraft lower in the period 1650–1700 than in the period 1560–1650? (16 marks)

You may use the following in your answer and any other information of your own.

- Two new acts on witchcraft were passed in 1563 and 1604.
- The English Civil War broke out in 1642 and did not end until 1648.
- Charles II founded the Royal Society in 1663.

Student answer

There are two main reasons why the number of witchcraft trials declined in the last half of the 17th century. The first reason is that during the Civil Wars from 1642 to 1648, there was much upheaval and confusion. The best example of this confusion is shown by the case of Matthew Hopkins, who became known as the 'Witchfinder General'. From 1644 until 1647, he and his assistants went around the counties of East Anglia and soon, a mass hysteria about witches and witchcraft developed. When the Civil War came to an end, his activities stopped.

The other main reason why the number of trials declined after 1650 was because the second half of the 17th century saw important developments in science and the understanding of the natural world. More educated people began to lose their traditional beliefs in magic and superstition. It was the educated classes who acted as magistrates and judges. They thus became less likely to hold trials, or to find people guilty if a trial went ahead.

Examiner comments

This answer gives some relevant and precise own knowledge about two important explanations, and it is clearly focused on the question. Each of the points made is well supported by factual evidence and the answer nearly reaches level four. However, the answer misses out some other important reasons for the difference in the two periods. These would be needed if full marks are to be gained.

To push this up to the top level and so gain full marks, the student could comment on the dates given in the bullet points for witchcraft acts and the attitudes of the authorities at those times; the attitude of Charles II to scientific approaches; the significance of religious and political conflicts, and their decline; and social and economic developments.

Extract from an improved student answer

There are several reasons why the number of witchcraft trials were lower after 1650, than in 1560–1650. In the first part of the period 1560–1650, most people believed in witches; even King James I and the authorities were very concerned about witchcraft. This explains why new acts were passed in 1563 and 1604 and accusations increased.

Another reason for the increase was the religious and political upheavals before and during the Civil War of 1642–1649. These allowed people like Matthew Hopkins (the so-called 'Witchfinder General') to carry out his witch-hunts. The decline in accusations after 1650 was because, for most people, the economic and social situation began to improve, so people were looking less for scapegoats to blame.

The other main reason why the number of trials declined after 1650 was the significant developments in science which led to an improved understanding of the natural world. This meant people could explain what had before appeared magical. A more rational approach was encouraged by the changing attitudes of people in authority, such as Charles II who supported scientific discoveries. More and more of the magistrates and judges who enforced the laws were less likely to hold witch trials or to find people guilty if a trial went ahead.

Protest, law and order in the twentieth century

Introduction

In this unit you will explore four case studies of important protests that took place during the last century. Two of these case studies will be about political protests:

- the suffragettes' campaign for votes for women, 1903–14
- the poll tax protests, 1990.

The other two case studies are about economic protests:

- the General Strike of 1926
- the miners' strike of 1984–85.

As well as finding out about the main events, you will be asked to think about the importance of factors such as leadership, organisation, the media, the powers of governments, and how these contributed to the success or failure of these protests.

Aims and outcomes

Unit 3 of the specification is a Source Enquiry. By the end of this section, you should be able to complete the following source skills:

- inference and portrayal
- source analysis
- source evaluation for reliability or utility
- cross referencing of sources
- using sources and own knowledge to make a judgement.

Activity

1 Get into groups of four or five.

Look at Source A, which shows protesters running away from a police charge during the miners' strike of 1984–85. Then take 5–10 minutes to discuss the following questions:

(a) The government has a lot of power to use against protesters. Do you think protests ever win against governments? If so, how?

(b) If you were to protest for or against something, how far would you be prepared to go? Would you be prepared to break the law, or even risk injury or death?

Now share your group's ideas with the rest of your class.

The General Strike, 1926

The *Constitution*

A "PLEBS" STRIKE CARTOON.
THE ELEPHANT: *"Ooh! I must be careful not to tread on THAT!!"*

The General Strike saw massive support from workers against the government, yet union leaders called off the strike because they wanted to work within the democratic tradition, not crush it.

Source A: This scene from the miners' strike shows strikers fleeing a police charge. Was it typical or even fully reliable? The miners' strike saw plenty of violence on both sides. Can violence in pursuit of a cause ever be justified? Is state violence always acceptable?

Suffragettes

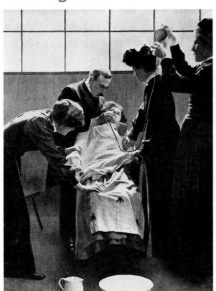

An imprisoned suffragette being force-fed. Do you think there is any cause for which you would be prepared to risk such suffering?

Poll tax protests

Protesters burning their poll tax bills in public. This was one of the peaceful forms of protests used. Is this type of peaceful civil disobedience an effective way to protest? What are the strong and weak points about it as a way of protesting?

6.1 Suffragettes: the early years, 1903–06

Women and the right to vote

By the late 19th century, women still had very few rights – in particular, they remained without the vote in general elections. There had been some progress in gaining equality for women in education, the law and local government, but women who wanted the vote faced big problems. Most people, women included, thought that politics was something that should be left to men.

More importantly, women campaigning for the right to vote had no real power. So how could such a powerless group of 'outsiders' persuade those with political power to share it with them? Eventually, some women began to argue that they would have to adopt the militant tactics used earlier by men when they were struggling for the right to vote.

Key factors affecting the suffragettes' protest

Many factors influenced the nature of the struggle for women's suffrage/the right to vote.

- **Attitudes of the authorities:** political protest was allowed as long as it was within the law and did not cause political embarrassment. How effective was peaceful protest in this case?
- **Publicity:** the suffragettes were very successful in getting media attention but it was not always favourable to their cause.
- **Decisions made by leaders:** the way the protest was organised and led was also crucial. Political organisations often disagree over the best way to achieve goals, and protests often split down moderate and radical lines between those prepared to work with the system and those who are not.

Source A: Emmeline, Christabel and Sylvia Pankhurst, the main leaders of the WSPU, together with two other important suffragettes.

Organisation and leadership: the suffragettes begin

In 1897, several regional women's suffrage groups came together to form the National Union of Women's Suffrage Societies (NUWSS). These suffragists, led by Millicent Fawcett, believed in peaceful protest and was prepared to work with politicians (men, of course) to achieve their goals. They wrote letters to newspapers and MPs, produced leaflets, got signatures on petitions and held peaceful demonstrations to persuade MPs to support them.

By the beginning of the 20th century, despite their best efforts, women were still unable to vote in parliamentary elections. Many suffragists became increasingly impatient with these unsuccessful peaceful methods. In 1903, Emmeline Pankhurst and her daughters Christabel and Sylvia set up the Women's Social and Political Union (WSPU). Its motto was 'Deeds, not Words'. Its members soon became known as the 'suffragettes' – a nickname given to them by the *Daily Mail* – to avoid any confusion with the older and more peaceful NUWSS.

Source B: An extract from Emmeline Pankhurst, *My Own Story*, 1914. Here she is describing the aims of the WSPU.

> To secure for women the Parliamentary vote as it is or may be granted to men. To limit our membership to women and to be satisfied with nothing but action on our question. 'Deeds, not Words' was to be our motto.
>
> Our members are absolutely single-minded; they concentrate all their forces on one object, political equality with men. No member of the WSPU divides her attention between suffrage and other social reforms.

One of the most important aspects of the WSPU leadership was to organise events that got them publicity for their cause. Their actions – whether it was disrupting political meetings, chaining themselves to railings or destroying property – put their campaign on the front pages of the newspapers.

Activities

Study Source B.

1 What can you learn about the WSPU from this source? Explain your answer.

2 In what way was the WSPU different from other organisations campaigning for the vote for women?

3 What do you think were the main problems facing women in their campaigns to get equal voting rights with men?

For discussion

4 Given the problems faced by women in trying to get the right to vote, do you think the methods of the NUWSS were correct? What might be the possible consequences of women taking more direct action?

 ResultsPlus

Watch out!

Students often just rephrase the source in their answers. Students who do well will work out what the source implies. For example, what do the words 'Deeds, not Words' suggest? You could say they suggest that the WSPU felt that the earlier movements had not been active enough. This will get you the higher marks.

Summary

- Different factors affect the causes, leaders and tactics of protest.
- At the start of the 20th century, women did not have the right to vote (suffrage).
- Earlier suffrage groups had tried peaceful methods to influence political opinion.
- The suffragette movement was started because of frustration that the peaceful methods of the suffragists had not achieved the vote for women.

6.2 Suffragettes: developments, 1906–08

Learning outcomes

By the end of this topic you should be able to:

● find out about the methods used by the suffragettes in the period 1906–08

● discover how this affected relations with the NUWSS.

When the Liberals won a landslide victory in the 1906 election, many thought women would soon get the vote. Many Liberal MPs supported rights for women, but the new government said that other reforms were more urgent than women's suffrage. In 1908, Asquith became Prime Minister. He told suffrage groups to prove there was popular support for the idea.

Protest and publicity, 1906–08

Faced with this challenge, the moderate National Union of Women's Suffrage Societies (NUWSS) and the more radical Women's Social and Political Union (WSPU) set out to gain popular support with publicity events and to demonstrate this support to the government.

● Thousands of leaflets were given out: the WSPU even dropped them from airships. There was also a suffragette newspaper, called *Votes for Women*, which suffragettes sold in the street.

● Women staged 'publicity stunts' to raise public awareness and advertise meetings.

● Both the WSPU and the NUWSS held large demonstrations in London, with supporters coming from all over the country. In 1907, the NUWSS attracted over 3,000 women to a march in London (known as the 'Mud March' because of the bad weather). The WSPU march to Hyde Park in June 1908 had over 300,000 protesters, with brass bands playing suffragette songs.

● The WSPU also took more radical steps to put pressure on the government. In October 1906, WSPU members broke the law by protesting in the House of Commons. They were arrested and sent to prison. WSPU members also chained themselves to the railings outside Downing Street and government buildings.

Source A: Members of the WSPU demonstrating on a boat on the River Thames, opposite the House of Commons. Note the banner advertising their planned demonstration for June 1908.

Source B: The great 'Votes for Women' demonstration held in Hyde Park on 21 June 1908, organised by the suffragettes. Marchers came from all over Britain.

However, Asquith still did nothing about votes for women. The NUWSS continued to believe that the best chance of getting votes for women was to stay close to the Liberal Party and its MPs, but the WSPU decided to step up their campaign with more dramatic methods of protest. The NUWSS were worried by this increasing militancy, and the two groups started to split away from each other.

Source C: A member of the WSPU who had chained herself to railings outside the House of Commons. This tactic meant that the police found it difficult to remove them, so the women had more time to make their protests heard and seen.

Source D: An extract from the *Daily Mirror* in 1906.

When the suffragettes began their campaign they were mistaken for featherheads, flibbertigibbets. Now that they have proved that they are in dead earnest, they have frightened the government, they have broken through the law, they have made 'Votes for women' practical politics.

Activities

1 Study Sources A, B and C. How do you think (a) the public, (b) the media and (c) the authorities of the time might have reacted to each of these tactics?

For discussion

2 If you had supported votes for women in 1906, would you have supported the NUWSS or the WSPU? Give several reasons for your answer.

ResultsPlus
Build better answers

What can you learn from Source D about suffragette tactics? (6 marks)

■ **Basic, Level 1 (1 mark)**
Answer takes information from the source, for example, 'they broke the law'.

● **Good, Level 2 (2–3 marks)**
Answer makes correct inference(s), for example, 'they made people change their mind about the suffragettes' but does not give details from the source to support them.

▲ **Excellent, Level 3 (4–6 marks)**
Answer makes supported inference(s), for example: 'Their tactics made people change their mind about the suffragettes. The *Daily Mirror* now thinks they are not 'featherheads', but a group who can make people take votes for women seriously – making it practical politics.'

Summary

- The new Liberal government of 1906 was expected to give women the vote, but it didn't; instead, it asked for more evidence of popular support.
- Women's suffrage groups used many different tactics to get publicity and public support.
- The government continued to resist and the WSPU decided to step up its campaign.
- The moderate NUWSS did not agree with the WSPU's more militant tactics and the two groups split.

6.3 Suffragettes: government attempts to deal with the protest

Learning outcomes

By the end of this topic you will be able to:

- find out about the increased militancy adopted by the WSPU
- discover how the government tried to cope with the protests.

The government found it very difficult to deal with the suffragette protest without upsetting public opinion and encouraging more support for the suffragettes.

Mixed messages

The Liberal government didn't have one clear view on votes for women. Some of its members supported the cause, others opposed it or weren't decided. Several times, the government seemed about to introduce a reform to extend the vote to some women but, each time, it was withdrawn or altered.

Shutting out peaceful protest

Once the WSPU became more militant, however, the government decided to take a hard line. When women disrupted political meetings by heckling or other forms of peaceful protest, the government responded by banning all women from Liberal meetings. This closed off an important avenue of peaceful protest.

Use of prisons

WSPU militants started a new tactic of breaking windows and refusing to pay fines so they could be sent to prison. The government refused to treat them as political prisoners and, instead, they were treated as ordinary criminals. This included not being allowed to speak and having to empty their chamber pots each morning. The government wanted to frighten and humiliate suffragettes so that they would stop this tactic. They did not want to encourage other groups looking for reform to try the same tactics or to recognise suffragette tactics as political protest.

Hunger strikes and force-feeding

When the government refused to treat them as political prisoners, some suffragettes went on hunger strike. This tactic put a lot of pressure on the government. If a woman starved herself to death in prison for a political cause, there would have been a storm of publicity and criticism of the government's handling of the issue. It would have created a martyr, increasing support for the suffragette cause.

So, the prison authorities began to force-feed these hunger-striking suffragettes. This meant pushing a tube down the throat and feeding watery gruel into the stomach. When a suffragette resisted, the prison warders sometimes used wedges to force their mouth open, or pushed a tube down through their nose. Many protesters vomited as soon as the tube was withdrawn. Occasionally, the gruel went into the lungs rather than the stomach. This caused serious health problems. Many WSPU prisoners suffered health problems as a result of their treatment in prison.

Source A: A WSPU poster of 1909, protesting against the force-feeding of suffragette prisoners on hunger strike.

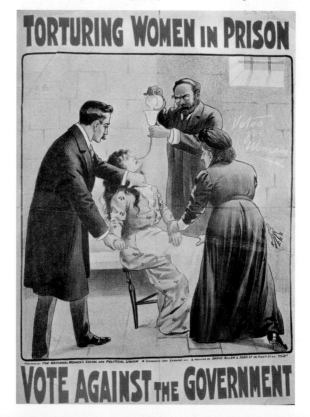

However, once details of the methods used had been publicised by the WSPU – for instance, in their paper *Votes for Women* – there was a public outcry. The suffragettes had succeeded in making the prison protests political.

Attempts at compromise

All protests involve a balance of power. If authorities are powerful enough to squash a protest, it gets nowhere. If protesters manage to get media opinion on their side, or if a government is afraid to use all the power it has against the protest because of what public reaction would be, then protesters can sometimes force change.

In 1910 Asquith agreed to work with the WSPU and the NUWSS to produce a Conciliation Bill, which would extend the right to vote to women. The WSPU agreed to a political truce and called off its violent protests. The two sides had reached a compromise and it seemed that progress was being made. However, the Liberals thought that women would vote for the Conservatives and the Conciliation Bill was abandoned.

The police and 'Black Friday'

The suffragettes were furious and, on Friday, 18 November 1910, over 300 went to parliament to protest. The government had instructed the police to frighten and humiliate the suffragettes so that they would stop their protests. There were many accusations of violent and even sexual assault

Source B: A suffragette struggling with a policeman on 'Black Friday', 18 November 1910.

by police on women. Twenty-nine women later complained of indecent assault by the police.

The result was that hundreds of suffragettes were now prepared to break windows and go to prison. Emmeline Pankhurst called the WSPU an 'army' and the suffragettes 'warriors'. From 1911, the suffragettes began a massive window-breaking campaign, along with the destruction of golfing greens – all designed to generate publicity.

The 'Cat and Mouse' Act

In 1913, the government passed the so-called 'Cat and Mouse' Act, which allowed the authorities to release a hunger-striker before they became seriously ill, and then re-arrest them once they had regained strength, in order to complete their sentence. This showed the government using its power to make laws to foil the protest and blunt the hunger-strike weapon.

Summary

- The government gave signals that reform was possible, but did nothing, infuriating suffrage groups.
- The government used the police and prison authorities against militant suffragettes who simply intensified their tactics.
- Suffragette publicity meant a lot of media attention, and a lot of pressure on the government.

6.4 Suffragettes and the media

Learning outcomes

By the end of this topic you should be able to:

- consider how the media reacted to the suffragette protest
- explore how successfully the suffragettes used the media to promote their cause.

The death of Emily Davison

At the 1913 Derby horse race, suffragette Emily Davison tried to stop the king's horse as a protest that would be seen by the royal family and all the world's media. Sadly, she was knocked down and her skull was fractured by the horse's hooves. Three days later, she died without ever regaining consciousness. The suffragette leaders didn't know that she was planning this protest. No one knows to this day whether she meant just to stop the horse or whether she intended to be run down by it.

At first, the media and the general public were angry at what seemed a pointless death from an irresponsible act. However, the WSPU organised two massive funerals for her, one in London and one in Morpeth, her home town. They made her a martyr for the cause of votes for women.

The death of Emily Davison illustrates some important themes in the suffragette protest. Only a small number of women were ever involved in the violent campaign for women's suffrage, yet the suffragettes managed to get massive media interest in their campaign (which meant newspaper coverage at this time). Why was this?

- Women breaking the law and being arrested and imprisoned was dramatic.
- Edwardian society valued modest, decent women who were happy to serve as wives and mothers. Suffragettes were shocking to many and made for good newspaper stories as a result.
- The suffrage movement put the government under pressure and this was interesting to newspaper readers.
- Newspapers themselves were for or against women's suffrage.
- The authorities used violence against newspapers that supported women.
- The suffragettes were very good at publicity – their tactics were always designed to get newspaper coverage.

Some newspapers were always totally against the call for women to be given the vote. This was especially true of *The Times*, which often ran articles and editorials condemning the campaign, even before the WSPU began to damage property.

Source A: The front page of the *Daily Sketch*, 8 June 1913.

Source B: An extract from *The Times*, 1912.

The suffragettes are a regrettable by-product of our civilisation, out with their hammers and their bags full of stones because of dreary, empty lives and high-strung, over-excitable natures.

Not all newspapers had this attitude to the principle of votes for women all the time.

- When campaigners restricted themselves to non-violent methods, there was often support for them in some newspapers.
- When the reactions of the police seemed unnecessarily violent or inappropriate (as on 'Black Friday'), some newspapers, such as the *Daily Mirror*, reported the incidents and published several photographs.
- The magazine *Punch* generally supported women's suffrage because it thought the Liberal government had done such a bad job in tackling the issue.

Source C: An extract from *The Daily Chronicle*, 1911, before the WSPU began its more violent methods.

> With sure and certain steps the cause of women's suffrage is marching to victory. Saturday's remarkable procession in London served as a prelude to the inevitable triumph. This peaceful pageant was one of the most impressive demonstrations that London has ever witnessed.

However, by and large the newspapers were against votes for women and were hostile to the suffragettes' tactics. What is interesting is that newspapers only really gave serious coverage to women's suffrage when the suffragettes started using violent tactics. So, even though the newspapers might be critical of the violent methods, they still gave the suffragettes what they wanted – publicity.

How successful was the suffragettes' use of the media?

If most media coverage of the suffragettes was negative, did that mean their campaign had failed? It is fair to say that what the suffragettes were trying to achieve was attention, and it didn't really matter whether it was positive or negative.

For the WSPU, though, the aim was to force change by exploiting every opportunity to put pressure on the government. This brought negative media coverage, and also their most militant tactics meant that the WSPU began to lose members to the NUWSS. Many important men tried to dismiss the suffragettes by claiming that those involved in such violent activities were mentally unstable or hysterical. Although public opinion was often hostile to the suffragettes, they kept the media's attention.

Activities

Study Sources A, B and C.

1 How does Source A cover Emily Davison's action (remember she died three days after the accident, so was still alive when the story was written)? What inferences can you draw from the main heading (the word 'wonderful', for example) about the way the media responded to the suffragette campaign as a whole?

2 Source A is from the *Daily Sketch*. Would you say this newspaper was closer to the viewpoint of Source B or Source C, or somewhere in between? Explain your answer by referring to both sources and the information on this page.

For discussion

3 Do you think the actions of the suffragettes helped or hindered their cause?

Summary

- The media gave lots of coverage to the suffragettes' actions for many different reasons, but perhaps most of all because the stories sold newspapers.
- The suffragettes designed their actions to get newspaper headlines.
- Newspaper coverage was broadly hostile to the suffragettes, with some exceptions.
- Newspaper coverage, positive or negative, fuelled the protest and put pressure on the government to respond.

6.5 Suffragettes: the end of the campaign

Learning outcomes

By the end of this topic you should be able to:

- explain the outcomes of the suffragettes' campaign
- consider the key factors affecting their protest.

In 1918, the Representation of the People Act gave votes to women householders, or women married to householders, over the age of 30 (men had to be over 21). It was not until 1928 that all women over the age of 21 were given the vote. Between the most militant phase of the suffragette protest in 1913–14 and 1918, the First World War occurred, in which vast numbers of women went to work while men fought on the battlefields. How did war affect the suffragette protest and the stalemate between the government and the protesters?

War and truce

In August 1914, all WSPU protests were suspended because of the outbreak of war with Germany. The WSPU then encouraged its members to support the war effort, despite the fact that women were still without the vote. They felt they could not engage in activities that would weaken the government at a time of national emergency. In return, the government released all WSPU prisoners so they could help with the war effort. The NUWSS followed suit, but did not support the war as enthusiastically as did most WSPU leaders.

Before the war, the government had been facing growing protest and disruption as a result of the suffragette campaign to get votes for women. During the war, women played an extremely important and active part in the war effort. Women were obviously capable of doing 'men's work'. They had made a huge contribution to Britain winning the war. Did this mean that society would now view them as worthy of the vote?

Splits in the suffragette leadership

Not all the suffrage groups supported the war and there were also tensions in the suffragette leadership. While suffragette leaders Emmeline and Christabel Pankhurst helped to recruit young men to serve in the war, Sylvia Pankhurst strongly opposed the war. She was a socialist and pacifist, and had left the WSPU in 1913 to form the East London Federation for working-class women, as she felt the WSPU was too focused on middle-class women.

In its early days, the WSPU had concentrated on getting the support of working-class women. Sylvia

Source A: Four female mechanics work on a car engine during the First World War. Women showed they could do 'men's work' in the war and thus challenged social attitudes to women's role in society.

wanted all women to have the vote, but Christabel wanted to appeal to the more prosperous members of society, and pointed out that the WSPU relied heavily on the money supplied by wealthy women. So she argued for a limited suffrage that would only give the vote to women with money and property. It was also Christabel who gave most support to the militant tactics, and finally went to France so she could organise the increasingly militant campaign from there, without fear of arrest and imprisonment.

Source B: Comments made in 1913 by Lloyd George, a senior minister in the Liberal government.

> Haven't the suffragettes the sense to see that the very worst way of campaigning for the vote is to try to intimidate or blackmail a man into giving them what he would gladly give otherwise?

Activities

1 Study Sources A and B. What evidence is there that the role of women in the war finally allowed men to 'gladly give' women the vote?

2 'Violent protest was the worst way of campaigning for the vote.' Do you agree? Use the sources and information on pages 112–115 to explain your decision.

ResultsPlus
Top tip!

When you explain your answer to questions such as Activity 2, always back up your answer using the sources and other information.

What was the outcome of the suffragette protest?

Historians dispute whether the war led directly to votes for women. Although women from all parts of society went to work, only women over 30 who were householders or wives of householders got the vote – the very people that Christabel Pankhurst wanted to influence through the suffragettes' campaign.

Many think that the same women who had led the women's suffrage movement, who had learned hard lessons about influencing governments, the media and public opinion, were responsible for grabbing the opportunity at the end of the war to push for suffrage. That would mean that the suffragettes and others had made the 1918 act possible.

Another linked view is that the war gave the government a way out of the stalemate: it couldn't crush this mass protest, but at the same time suffragettes couldn't get their way without government legislation. Also, the political situation had changed and each party was no longer worried that votes for women would deliver lots of new voters to their opposition. The new government did not want to return to all the problems of the suffragette protest, especially in view of emerging problems in Ireland and with trade unions.

Activities

3 Using the sources and the information from this topic, draw a diagram and answer the question below.

The government couldn't crush the protest, but the protesters couldn't get what they wanted without the government changing the law – the situation was like a balance. Draw a diagram to show the factors on either side of the balance of power. You could draw the most important factors as the heaviest 'weights'. What would you say tipped the balance of power to allow some women the vote?

Summary

- The First World War saw major changes in women's roles in society and was followed by an act giving some women the vote.

- The suffragettes ended their campaign during the war and actively supported the war effort.

- How important the suffragette tactics were in achieving votes for women is debatable, but most historians would not see the war as the only factor in achieving women's suffrage.

6.6 Source enquiry skills: making inferences

Learning outcomes

By the end of this topic you should be able to:

● demonstrate that a source can provide more information than is stated or shown

● understand how to make inferences from sources

● understand that details of a source create an overall image or message

● demonstrate an ability to analyse sources and show how an image has been created.

From information to inference

In History we often try to squeeze more information from a source than it actually tells us. For example, we like to know how people felt about big events as well as knowing what happened. Inference is the word used to describe something that can be worked out from a source, even though it is not actually stated or shown. The inference can be about the situation in the source or about the message that the author or artist wants to give.

Source A: A house attacked by suffragette arsonists in 1913. The house was owned by a Liberal MP.

The examination for Unit 3 will usually start with a question asking what you can learn from a source. It's asking you to make inferences.

For example, look at Source A below. What can you learn from Source A about the suffragette protests?

The source tells us that the suffragettes burnt this house, but you can go further than just giving that information. You can work out that some suffragettes were prepared to break the law as part of their protest. You could also make use of the information that it was a *Liberal* MP's house, which suggests that suffragettes were aiming to put pressure on the Liberal government.

Analysing sources

You can think about a historical source in the same way that you think about taking a photograph nowadays. To get the effect you want, you choose which things to focus on and which ones to leave out. When you analyse a source, break it into sections and look at each part separately in order to see what impression the artist or author is trying to give.

Small details can be very important. If you are looking at a picture source – for example, a portrait or a cartoon – you need to think about:

● what details have been included and why
● what is the centre of attention (and how has the artist made it the centre of attention?)
● whether anything has been deliberately missed out, etc.

For example, the poster on the opposite page, published by the suffragettes in 1913, is designed to turn voters against the government.

Note the points in the boxes around Source B. They show that overall the poster portrays the government as acting harshly against suffragettes, and gives the message that people should not vote for a government that acts like this.

Source B: A poster published by the WSPU in 1913.

Large cat looking fierce (note the teeth and the expression in the eyes)

Suffragette in centre, shown as small compared with the 'cat'

The words 'The Liberal Cat' show that this fierce animal represents the government that has passed the 'Cat and Mouse' Act

The message to the reader is to vote against the Liberal government

THE CAT AND MOUSE ACT
PASSED BY THE LIBERAL GOVERNMENT

THE LIBERAL CAT
ELECTORS VOTE AGAINST HIM
KEEP THE LIBERAL OUT!

BUY AND READ 'THE SUFFRAGETTE' PRICE 1D

Now read the points around Source C.

Source C: From Emmeline Pankhurst's' statement in court in 1908. Mrs Pankhurst was leader of the WSPU. Why do you think she has chosen to include this information?

The use of language to persuade people that her actions were right, e.g. 'duty to break the law' gives a positive view of her illegal actions. Can you find other examples from the source?

She chooses to describe other methods to show that peaceful methods have not worked: 'We have tried every way.'

We realise that it is our duty to break the law to call attention to why we break it.

We have tried every way. We have presented larger petitions than were ever presented before for any reform. We have held larger meetings than men have ever held for any reform. I come here not as a law breaker.

This is the only way women can get the power to decide on the laws we have to obey. We are here in this court not because we are law breakers; we are here in our efforts to become law-makers.

She chooses to include her reason for law breaking: 'to call attention'.

She emphasises how big the peaceful petitions and meetings were: 'larger petitions', 'larger meetings than men have ever held'.

Activity

1 Analyse Source C above. How does Emmeline Pankhurst portray her actions, and what message is she giving out?

Think about what things she has chosen to include and the words she has used.

Some examples have been done for you.

Summary

- Inferences can be worked out from a source even if they are not actually stated or shown in a visual source.
- Source analysis shows how something is portrayed and helps you to understand the message of a source.

7.1 The General Strike: the build-up

Learning outcomes

By the end of this topic you should be able to:

- outline the tensions between miners, mine owners and the government by 1925 and the reasons for them
- identify from sources the attitudes of the people who produced them.

One of the most spectacular examples of industrial struggle between government and trade unions in Britain occurred in 1926. This was the General Strike, during which over 2.5 million workers in many industries (including miners, transport workers, builders and printers) joined in a strike that lasted nine days. Despite the huge numbers on strike and the massive impact this had on the economy, the strike was called off after nine days. Why did the strike leaders release this stranglehold without achieving anything for the workers?

Tensions in the mining industry

The main causes of the General Strike were to do with the mining industry. There had long been problems between the private owners of the coalmines and the miners' unions. These had mainly been over safety and pay. In particular, increasing overseas competition meant that mine owners tried to maintain profits by cutting the wages and increasing the working day of the miners. Miners fought back with strikes. The government backed the mine owners and used the army and police to smash strikes. Coal was essential to the economy: without it, the country would have no heat or power.

Source A: A cartoon of 1925, criticising the mining union leader, Arthur Cook. Most of the press were anti-union and particularly singled him out for attacks. How does the cartoonist get his message across?

Strength in numbers

Strikes were organised by the unions, but there were different unions for different industries. When the three main unions of miners, transport workers and railwaymen formed the Triple Industrial Alliance (TIA), a major powerbase was created. The TIA was an agreement to strike together and not settle until all three unions had been able to obtain satisfactory agreements. If these industries stopped working, the country would grind to a halt. What would the unions do with this power?

War and government control

As happened with the suffragette protest, the First World War meant that priorities changed as the focus for everyone in Britain was on the war effort. Coal was an essential part of this. The government needed to ensure that coal production was continuously maintained at a high level. Therefore it nationalised the industry, taking control of the mines and paying the miners directly.

After the war – disappointment

The miners were paid well, kept safe and given high status as essential workers in the war effort. They hoped that the government would nationalise mining after the war, but despite a commission recommending this, the government returned control of the mines to their owners, who immediately drew up plans to cut wages and increase hours.

The miners went on strike in 1921 and the TIA agreed to support them. However, on Friday, 15 April, J.H. Thomas, leader of the railway union, refused to act on the very day the strike was supposed to begin. This event was known as 'Black Friday'. The miners' strike failed, after much suffering, but in 1925 the threat of a real TIA strike forced the Conservative government to give a nine-month subsidy to the private owners to prevent the wage cuts. This became known as 'Red Friday' (31 July 1925). The Samuel Commission was set up to investigate the problems of the mining industry.

The Samuel Commission's report

In April 1925, the employers made it clear that, once the subsidy came to an end, they would reduce wages by 10 per cent and increase the miners' hours from seven to eight a day – with no extra pay. The Samuel Commission suggested reforms, opposed the extra working hours, but also said that the miners should accept some wage cuts. The mine owners rejected these recommendations – as did the miners' union, saying 'Not a penny off the pay, not a minute on the day.'

Source B: A comment made in 1925 by Lord Birkenhead, a minister in the Conservative government.

> It would be possible to say without exaggeration that the miners' leaders were the stupidest men in England, if we had not had frequent occasion to meet the mine owners.

Activities

1. Study Source A. Which side of the dispute do you think the cartoon is supporting – the miners or the mine owners?

2. Study Source B. Does he support either side? Explain your answer.

ResultsPlus
Build better answers

Study Source A. How does the cartoonist get his message across? (8 marks)

■ **Basic, Level 1 (1–2 marks)**
Answer describes the cartoon, for example it will explain that Arthur Cook wanted 'not a penny off the pay'.

● **Good, Level 2 (3–5 marks)**
Answer identifies a message and links it to specific details from the source, for example, that Arthur Cook is not facing the 'hard economic facts' on the wall.

▲ **Excellent, Level 3 (6–8 marks)**
Answer demonstrates how the message is created by the cartoonist. The details on the wall and the use of 'you'd much better face it' are used to show that Arthur Cook's demands are not sensible and miners must face the economic facts.

Summary

- There were tensions and conflicts in the mining industry, between the owners and the miners, with governments sometimes sending in troops to end strikes.

- During the First World War, the miners had been pleased when the government took temporary control of the mines. They were angry when the mines were returned to the control of the mine owners.

- The recommendation of the Samuel Commission on pay and hours in mining in 1925 pleased neither the owners nor the miners.

7.2 The General Strike: government tactics

Learning outcomes

By the end of this topic you should be able to:
- explain how the government prepared for a general strike
- analyse sources to work out the attitudes of their authors.

In the suffragette campaign, government responses often seemed badly thought out, allowing the protesters opportunities to use what the government said or did to their advantage. Government responses to the threat of a general strike were different. The stakes seemed so high that the government used the full range and power of its authority to combat this threat.

Attitudes towards socialism and communism

The Russian Revolution of 1917 was a huge worry for governments across the world. The Bolsheviks got the support of industrial workers with the promise of a communist state, with no private ownership of industry and an end to governments protecting the rich against the poor. Communist parties were gaining ground in many European countries, including Britain. The Conservative government was determined to prevent any attempt by workers to take power from the state.

Media responses

Some classes of British society were also very frightened of what the workers would do, and the media generally reflected and reinforced these concerns. Threats of a general strike were often portrayed as a threat to parliamentary democracy, to the institutions that made Britain what it was.

Buying time

The miners believed that the subsidies given by the government to prevent wage cuts meant that

Source A: A *Punch* cartoon from 1925, commenting on the subsidy to mine owners. The boy is Prime Minister Baldwin; the grown up is the British public, footing the £10 million bill.

the government was on their side. In fact, many in the government saw this as a temporary retreat in order to ensure victory in the battle against a general strike which, they felt sure, would come soon – they were giving themselves time to prepare. This was an important government tactic.

Source B: Comments about the subsidy made by Churchill, the Conservative Chancellor of the Exchequer, in the House of Commons in October 1925.

We therefore decided to postpone the crisis in the hope of averting it, of coping with it effectually when the time came.

Preparing for action

From 'Red Friday' onwards, the government began to put together the mechanisms to deal with a general strike.

- The country was divided into regions, with each one having permanent headquarters; a communications network was created between the London central headquarters and local authorities. Reactions to local events would be faster and easier to co-ordinate if many things happened at once.
- Resources were stockpiled, including food, and emergency electricity generation was organised – this would reduce the impact of a general strike for a few days.
- An officially independent Organisation for the Maintenance of Supplies (OMS) was set up in September 1925 to recruit and train 'volunteer labour' to act as strike-breakers. In reality, Churchill, the Chancellor of the Exchequer, oversaw this.
- Access to the media during the strike was organised, so the government could control what the public heard about the strike.
- The government used the 1920 Emergency Powers Act to recruit a large number of special constables to help the police deal with the strike.
- Plans were made for using the armed forces to maintain supplies, guard installations and to fight against strikers if required.

Source C: Tanks were ready in London to defend the government against attack during the General Strike.

Activities

1 Study Sources B and C. How do these sources show different government preparations against a general strike?
2 List the preparations the government made before the strike and describe the ways that each was intended to reduce the strike damage.

The start of the General Strike

After the miners announced 'Not a penny off the pay, not a minute on the day', mine owners closed all the pits to force the miners to accept the new conditions by causing real hardship. The unions were outraged. At first, the government seemed to be holding talks with unions to prevent a general strike, but the talks were ended by the government when some print workers on the *Daily Mail* refused to print an anti-strike editorial, even though union negotiators made it clear that this had been done without their backing.

Union negotiations had been led by the Trade Union Congress (TUC), the organisation representing all unions. The TUC leaders called a general strike in support of the miners for 4 May 1926.

Source D: An extract from the editorial in the *Daily Mail*, 3 May 1926, which union members refused to print.

A general strike is not an industrial dispute; it is a revolutionary movement, intended to inflict suffering upon the great mass of innocent persons in the community and thus to force its will upon the government. It is a movement that can only succeed by destroying government and undermining the rights and liberties of the people.

Summary

- The government was well prepared for a general strike by 1926.
- Its tactics included delaying the protest with compromise until it felt ready to defeat a general strike.

7.3 The General Strike, 4–12 May 1926

Learning outcomes

By the end of this topic you should be able to:

- explain what happened during the General Strike
- find out how the miners were affected after the General Strike was called off.

Unlike the government, the TUC did not use the time to plan the General Strike properly. It wanted workers to come out in stages, according to occupation, with public health, medical and food workers excluded from the strike so lives were not put at risk. Despite the lack of TUC organisation, millions of workers struck on the first day, including many from what the TUC wanted to be the second wave.

Media control

The government produced a paper, *The British Gazette* (edited by Churchill), attacking the General Strike as a threat to destroy the laws and the British Constitution itself, while the TUC's *British Worker* stressed that it was purely an industrial

Source A: The arrest of a striker in Hammersmith Broadway, after an attempt to prevent the passage of a milk lorry being driven by OMS volunteers. All such lorries had police escorts.

Source B: Police mounting a baton charge against strikers in Walworth, South London.

dispute. The TUC newspaper was only four pages long, as the government had taken over supplies of newsprint.

Although government ministers made frequent BBC broadcasts about the strike, the BBC refused to allow union leaders or the leader of the Labour Party to speak on the radio. Even the Archbishop of Canterbury, who favoured a compromise, was excluded until the strike was almost over. The BBC explained these restrictions by the fact that the courts had ruled that the General Strike was illegal.

Local actions

In many areas, the strike continued to grow and, in some areas, workers formed self-defence militias to control transport in their area, and to prevent police interference and the activities of the OMS volunteers. Although there were one or two clashes between the police and strikers – mostly in London, Newcastle and Glasgow – it was mainly peaceful. This was because in most areas, both the police and the strikers were anxious not to provoke any violent outbursts. However, over 5,000 strikers were arrested for alleged disorder, picketing or inciting others to join the strike.

The end of the General Strike

Despite the actions of the police and the OMS, the strike was very successful, and public transport came to a complete stop in many areas. Yet suddenly, after only nine days, the TUC called off the strike. They felt they were losing control of the strike: in many areas, local Councils of Action were set up to organise strikers. The TUC did not want to be involved with a strike that, according to the government and the courts, was a challenge to the elected parliament. This left the miners on their own and finally, in November 1926, they were forced back to work by hunger and poverty.

Source C: An extract from the records of the Women's Committee for the relief of Miners' Wives and Children, 1926.

In the last village [in the Leicester area] I visited two heartbroken mothers. One had a baby born on Sunday, for which she had been longing for years, and it had died on Monday. The district nurse said she could suggest no reason for its condition but the mother's weakness through lack of food.

Many who had participated were victimised and 'blacklisted', despite the government's promise that this would not happen. Many others had to sign a letter promising not to belong to a trade union. Consequently, trade union membership, which by 1919 had reached 7.9 million, fell to below 4 million in 1930.

In 1927, the Conservative government passed the Trades Disputes Act, which made all general and 'sympathy' strikes illegal.

Source D: In this cartoon, the TUC's attempt to 'roll over' the lawful state fails as the lever of the General Strike breaks under the strain.

THE LEVER BREAKS.

Summary

- Despite a lack of organisation and government efforts to keep the country going, the General Strike was very successful – millions joined in.
- The strike was largely peaceful.
- The TUC leadership called off the strike with nothing to show for it.

7.4 The General Strike: a failure of leadership?

124

While the numbers involved in the General Strike of 1926 were much higher than earlier general strikes in other countries, it ended without achieving any of its goals. This has often been explained by the fact that the leaders of the TUC had not wanted the strike in the first place, and tried to end it as quickly as possible once it had started.

TUC actions

While the government portrayed the General Strike as a deliberate attempt at revolution, the TUC leadership actually did all they could to prevent it. They did not urge the miners to strike: in fact, they put pressure on the miners to accept the wage cuts of up to 13 per cent that were recommended by the Samuel Commission. In the six weeks running up to the General Strike, the TUC made every effort to find a compromise – to secure an 'honourable settlement'.

Why were the TUC against the General Strike?

● TUC leaders didn't think it would work – it was such a challenge to the government that negotiations would be impossible.

● It would be seen as an attempt at revolution rather than an industrial dispute to improve conditions and the TUC didn't want a revolution.

● It was too big to control – if something went wrong, then public opinion would turn against the unions completely.

● The TUC thought the miners were not being realistic about the economic situation.

● They were worried about the new Communist Party, set up in 1921, which was encouraging unofficial actions and breakaway local councils.

TUC leadership during the strike

The TUC leadership repeatedly stressed that this was an industrial dispute and not an attack on the state. They wanted the strike to be peaceful and lawful, so as not to alarm the public or damage their ability to negotiate with the government. The TUC had so much to lose from the strike that they ended it in humiliating circumstances.

Source A: Comments made by Walter Citrine, General Secretary of the TUC, during the General Strike.

> A general strike… is a literal impossibility… In some imperfect way services essential to life must be carried on.

Militant trade unionists claimed, and still claim, that such 'leadership' meant that the General Strike was seriously weakened right from the start.

Source B: Part of a message issued to all workers by the TUC in the *British Worker*.

> The General Council of the Trades Union Congress wishes to emphasise the fact that this is an industrial dispute… The outbreak of any disturbances would be very damaging to the prospects of a successful termination to the dispute.
>
> The Council asks pickets especially to avoid obstruction and to confine themselves strictly to their legitimate duties.

Source C: The front page of the first edition of the *British Worker* of 5 May 1926.

THE BRITISH WORKER

OFFICIAL STRIKE NEWS BULLETIN

Published by The General Council of the Trades Union Congress

No. 1.   WEDNESDAY EVENING, MAY 5, 1926.   PRICE ONE PENNY

IN LONDON AND THE SOUTH

Splendid Loyalty of Transport Workers

EVERY DOCKER OUT

" London dock workers are absolutely splendid," said an official

WONDERFUL RESPONSE TO THE CALL

General Council's Message : Stand Firm and Keep Order

The workers' response has exceeded all expectations. The

SOUTH WALES IS SOLID !

Not a Wheel Turning in Allied Industries

'MEN ARE SPLENDID !'

Throughout South Wales the stoppage is complete, and every-

Was the General Strike political?

The government's message was clear: the General Strike was an attack on the state. The TUC leadership weren't looking for a revolution, but they were not in full control of strikers. In many areas, strikers ignored the TUC and set up Councils of Action to co-ordinate strike action; some even took over the distribution of food to local people. Local union militants attacked the TUC for trying to keep union members at work (the TUC didn't want everyone to strike all at once) and, in areas where violence broke out between strikers and the police or strike breakers, Workers Defence Corps were set up to protect picket lines. The newly formed Communist Party of Great Britain was often involved: was this the revolution the government warned of?

Source D: Various comments made in the *British Gazette* during the General Strike.

(i) … Either the nation must be mistress in its own house, or suffer the existing constitution to be fatally injured and endure the growth of a Soviet of Trade Unions.

(ii) Either the country will break the General Strike or the General Strike will break the country.

Activities

1 What do Sources A, B and C tell us about the attitude of most TUC leaders to the General Strike?

2 Do you think the TUC leaders were right to treat the General Strike as a problem rather than an opportunity?

3 Read Source D. Why do you think the government published these comments, which portrayed the strike as a revolutionary threat?

For discussion

4 Do you think the General Strike was a political or an industrial dispute?

Summary

- The TUC leadership thought a general strike would damage union power, not increase it.
- Although the scale of the protest was enormous, local militant leadership was not strong enough to overcome the massive government operation in the long term.

7.5 Source enquiry skills: reliability of sources

Learning outcomes

By the end of this topic you should be able to:

- understand that sources are not completely reliable
- explain the factors affecting the reliability of a source
- evaluate the reliability of a source.

Before any source can be used, the historian always needs to evaluate its reliability by considering the following:

Reliability of sources

Content of the source – Do any details suggest the author or artist was an eyewitness or has detailed and accurate knowledge of what happened?

Language – Is the language loaded in any way? Are there any words that suggest the author feels so strongly that he might not give an accurate account?

Origins – Who was the author/artist? Was he involved? Where does his knowledge come from? When and where did he produce the source?

Purpose – Why was this source produced? Was the author/artist paid to produce it? Is it a celebration? Is it intended as a factual record, or even as a joke? Was there any reason why the author might not include certain details?

Nature – What sort of source is it? Can private sources such as a diary or letter be trusted? Are government statistics likely to be accurate? Do newspapers always sensationalise their reports?

Selection – What details has the author/artist chosen to put in? What has been missed out? How does that affect the overall impression the source creates in your mind?

An important thing to remember in your answer is to focus on the specific source. Newspapers may sometimes exaggerate their accounts in order to make them interesting and sell more copies, but this is not a relevant comment unless you can provide examples from this specific source. Consider Source A:

Source A: An extract from the first edition of the *British Gazette*, produced by the government on 4 May 1926.

> The great strike began yesterday. There are already many signs, however, that it is by no means so complete as its promoters hoped.

Source A is from an unusual newspaper. It was produced by the government during the strike, but you should not just assume that this will make it unreliable. Can you find evidence in the source itself? The article says the 'strike is by no means… complete'. This might be because the government wanted to convince the readers that the strike was not successful. It doesn't give you percentages. Something with 99 per cent support would be well supported, but not complete.

Biased sources

A source is also likely to reflect the opinion of the author – not many people would bother to write about an event if they didn't have some sort of opinion about it! But that doesn't mean the source is automatically unreliable. You need to decide if the writer's feelings are so strong and their account is so one-sided that the source cannot be trusted, in which case it is biased. Remember that if you say a source is biased you must always explain how that bias affects the account (for example, biased in favour of the strikers and praising their organisation and good behaviour, or biased against them and choosing to highlight incidents of violence or strike-breaking). You also have to be able to back up your comments with evidence of loaded language, exaggerations or factual inaccuracies.

Source B: An extract from *Britain Since 1700*, R.J. Cootes, 1982.

> Considering the serious nature of the dispute, most people were remarkably peaceful and good-humoured. At Plymouth, for instance, a team of strikers played the local police at soccer… Foreign observers were greatly impressed by the calmness of the British people. The *Philadelphia Record*, an American newspaper, pointed out on 11 May that after a week of the greatest industrial dispute in the nation's history 'not a single life has been lost, not a single shot fired'.

The author is making a comment in favour of the strikers. The peacefulness and the lack of violence is emphasised, but that does not mean the source is biased. The author is able to look back at this strike and use evidence from many sources. You might want to check whether there was violence – but note that the source does not claim there was no violence at all. He says 'Most people were… peaceful'. There is no reason to think that this source is unreliable, even though it was written nearly 60 years later and is sympathetic to the strikers.

Activities

1 Explain why each of the following is not automatically reliable:

   • a photograph

   • an eyewitness account.

2 Explain how an account written 60 years after an event can still be a reliable source.

3 Look back at Source B on page 124. How reliable do you think it is? Explain your answer.

ResultsPlus
Build better answers

Study Source A on page 122 and Source B on page 127. How reliable are these sources as evidence of the way the strikers behaved during the strike? Explain your answer using these sources. (10 marks)

■ **Basic, Level 1 (1–3 marks)**
Answer gives undeveloped comments, for example assuming that Source A is more reliable because it is from the time of the strikes.

● **Good, Level 2 (4–7 marks)**
Answer gives detailed comments using the content or nature of Sources A and B, noting for example that Source A can be relied upon as visual evidence of that moment in time, in Hammersmith, after strikers obstructed a milk lorry, but that Source B says there was little violence generally.

▲ **Excellent, Level 3 (8–10 marks)**
Answer will evaluate the sources, considering their nature and content. Answer may mention, for example, that Source B is based on the author's enquiry into records of events and into newspapers published at the time, and can be relied upon to give a more general impression of the levels of violence than Source A can. The answer would go on to support this comment using both of the sources.

Summary

• The reliability of a source is affected by a range of different factors, and very few sources are totally reliable or totally unreliable. However, you should not assume that sources written after an event are less reliable than those written at the time.

• In the examination, you need to decide how far a source is reliable, *and* to be able to show how you reached your judgement.

7.6 Source enquiry skills: cross-referencing sources

Learning outcomes

By the end of this topic you should be able to:

- show understanding that the accuracy of a source can be checked by comparing it to other sources
- identify points of similarity and of difference when sources are compared
- weigh up the similarities and differences in order to reach a judgement on accuracy.

Source A: An extract from the first edition of the *British Gazette*, published by the government on 5 May 1926.

> The great strike began yesterday. There are already many signs, however, that it is by no means so complete as its promoters hoped.

Source B: Part of a statement issued by the General Council of the TUC on 4 May 1926, the first day of the strike.

> We have reports from all over the country that have been much better than we hoped for. Not only the railwaymen and transport men, but all other trades came out on strike in a way we did not expect immediately.

Source C: An extract from the first edition (5 May 1926) of the *British Worker*, produced by the TUC.

> The workers' response was better than we hoped for.... All the essential industries and all the transport services have been brought to a standstill.

Historians frequently compare and cross-reference sources to check their accuracy. For example, Source C from the *British Worker*, gives the impression that the strike is so successful that most major industries are at a standstill. How far do sources A and B support this impression?

Cross-referencing sources

When you cross-reference sources, you need to follow certain steps to make sure it is done properly:

- Have a clear idea of what it is you want to check in the first source (list the details you are checking).
- Check the other sources to see what they say about each of those details. Are they confirmed, challenged or just not mentioned?
- Look at the differences. Are they small differences (e.g. in numbers), or big differences that might even contradict each other?
- What attitude is shown in the sources? Do they show any bias which you will need to take into account?
- Weigh up the similarities and differences between the sources.

It can be helpful to draw a table (like the one opposite), especially if you are cross-referencing more than two sources; then you can compare the sources and see how much support there is for each point.

Next, think about whether there are important differences in these three sources:

- Very few details are in complete agreement except that there actually was a strike.
- They suggest different levels of support for the strike.
- Only Source C talks about the effects as bringing essential industrial and transport services to a standstill.

You need to think about how far your conclusion is affected by the fact that Source A comes from the government, and Sources B and C are from the *British Worker* published by the TUC.

Details in Source A	Details in Source B	Details in Source C	Are details supported, challenged or not mentioned?
The strike is by no means so complete as its promoters hoped.	The reports of the strike were better than we hoped for.	The workers' response was better than we hoped for.	Source C is directly challenged by Source A, but directly supported by Source B.
The great strike began yesterday (4 May).	The railwaymen, transport men and all other trades have come out (4 May).	All essential industries and all the transport services have been brought to a standstill (4 May).	They all agree that a strike began. Source B agrees that transport workers and other trades went on strike. Source A says 'great strike' so we can infer that it involved a lot of workers.
Transport services are not mentioned.	Standstill is not mentioned but refers to railwaymen and transport men out on strike.	Transport services have been brought to a standstill.	Does not mean Source C is unreliable on this point, but the detail about 'standstill' is not supported. A historian would need to check this against other sources.

Therefore, your conclusion might be:

Overall the three accounts agree that a strike began. Together they suggest that huge numbers went out on strike. Where they differ is that Source A chooses to highlight those who did not respond, while Sources B and C highlight the enthusiasm of those who did strike. It is difficult to know from these three sources how much support there was since Source A (a government paper) might want to give the impression that the strike did not have complete support, and Source B and C (from the TUC) might want to show that it was well supported. Although Source A does not mention the trades involved, it is likely that it was the transport workers because Sources B and C agree on this, and it is a factual detail easily checked. So we can conclude that the impression in C is accurate that a big strike involving transport workers began, although we cannot be certain that services were brought to a standstill.

Summary

- It is very rare to find a source that totally agrees with another, so you need to make a judgement about how far the second source backs up the first one.
- Cross-referencing should include a careful matching of detail, but should consider other issues of reliability too.

ResultsPlus
Build better answers

Study Sources A, B and C. How far do Sources B and C challenge the impression of the strike given in Source A? (10 marks)

■ **Basic, Level 1 (1–2 marks)**
Answer takes details from the source(s) or makes an accurate comment but does not support it with details from the source(s). For example, the answer may state that 'the sources disagree about the amount of strikers', but not say how or why.

● **Good, Level 2 (3–6 marks)**
Answer compares details from the sources to determine how far Sources B and C challenge Source A.

▲ **Excellent, Level 3 (7–10 marks)**
In addition to comparing details, the answer takes into account the nature of the sources when making a decision. For example, the answer may give examples from the sources to show that Sources B and C do not mention how complete the strike was, only that it was well supported, but Source A is taken from a government newspaper, emphasising that the strike was a disappointment to the organisers, and Sources B and C do challenge that directly.

8.1 The miners' strike: a trial of strength?

Learning outcomes

By the end of this topic you should be able to:

- explain how the miners' strike began in 1984 and how it was viewed by the leaders of both sides
- explain why the miners' strikes of the early 1970s defeated the Conservative government.

1970s: strong unions, weak governments

In the early 1970s, existing laws on union rights to call and organise strikes meant that governments had limited powers to prevent trade union action. In January 1972 and 1974 the miners went on strike over pay. They picketed mines and power stations. Other unions supported them, stopping fuel from being imported or transported. The Conservative government imposed a three-day working week to save power but was soon forced to agree to the miners' demands. In February 1974 the government was defeated in a general election over its handling of the unions.

These strikes show some key features that contributed to their success:

- they happened when coal was essential to industry
- the government couldn't get enough coal to power stations: the strikes stopped it being mined, transported or imported
- other unions supported the miners
- the strike happened in winter when demand for coal was highest.

New government leadership: Margaret Thatcher

In 1979 the Conservatives were back in power, led by Margaret Thatcher. Her authority was hugely increased by victory in the Falklands War in 1982 and re-election in 1983, and she had been in the 1974 Conservative government.

At the same time, coal mining was in serious trouble: it was cheaper to use oil, gas or coal from abroad. Many mines were classed as uneconomic – it cost more to get the coal out than it was worth as fuel. On 1 March 1984, a plan was announced to close 20 pits, with the loss of 20,000 jobs. The first pit to close was Cortonwood Colliery in South Yorkshire. This started the 1984–85 miners' strike.

Thatcher's government was determined to defeat the miners. The Conservatives were bitter about the way the miners' strikes had contributed to their defeat in the February 1974 election. Thatcher portrayed the struggle as another war, like the war in the Falklands. She said that giving in to the miners would be surrendering the rule of parliamentary democracy to the 'rule of the mob'.

Source A: An extract from Margaret Thatcher's speech in Parliament on 19 July 1984.

> We had to fight the enemy without [abroad] in the Falklands. We always have to be aware of the enemy within, which is much more difficult to fight and more dangerous to liberty.

Source B: Margaret Thatcher.

Activities

Study Source A.

1 What impression is it trying to put across about the striking miners?

2 What elements of the source help to give this impression?

Source C: Arthur Scargill, President of the NUM, on the picket line at Ollerton, 27 April 1984. Scargill is in the centre.

Miners' strike leadership: Arthur Scargill

Arthur Scargill was the leader of the National Union of Mineworkers (NUM). Following the news that 20 pits were to be closed, Scargill persuaded the rest of the NUM leadership to begin a national miners' strike. Under new laws it was illegal not to ballot workers before a strike, but Scargill argued that different areas had already voted for a strike, so a national ballot wasn't needed. Many miners were unhappy with this undemocratic process. For Scargill, though, it was a fight for survival.

Source D: An extract from Arthur Scargill's editorial in a special issue of *The Miner*, the NUM's official newspaper, March 1984.

I cannot emphasise enough that the Coal Board's ultimate intention is to wipe out half the South Notts coalfield, cut the Midlands area by forty per cent, close down half of the Scottish pits, cut the North Western Area's pits by half, close sixty per cent of collieries in the North East, wipe out half of North Derbyshire, seventy per cent of the pits in South Wales and shut down twenty Yorkshire collieries. No one can now say that he has not been warned.

Activities

3 How does Source D make the case for a national miners' strike?

4 Miners' strikes in 1972 and 1973 had been very effective, but the situation in 1984 was different. From the sources and information on these pages, what differences can you identify?

5 The 1984–85 miners' strike is often seen as a trial of strength between two leaders: Scargill and Thatcher. From what you know of other protests, what do you think each of these leaders should do next?

Summary

- The miners' strike of 1984–85 was about government plans to close uneconomic pits.

- Strikes had been very successful in the early 1970s, but in the 1980s the Conservative government was determined to end union power.

- The miners' leaders saw this strike as a battle for survival, not a negotiation for better conditions.

8.2 The miners' strike: tactics

Learning outcomes

By the end of this topic you should be able to:

- explain the tactics used on both sides of the miners' strike
- evaluate whether the government or the miners were stronger.

Source A: A mass picket of the night shift at Ollerton Colliery, Nottinghamshire, on 14 March 1984. Yorkshire miner David Jones was killed while picketing.

Source B: A miners' support group.

Source C: Extract from Arthur Scargill's response to clashes between strikers and police at Orgreave on 18 June 1984.

We've had riot shields, we've had riot gear, we've had police on horseback charging into our people, we've had people hit with truncheons and people kicked to the ground... The intimidation and the brutality that has been displayed are something reminiscent of a Latin American state.

The miners' tactics

- A national strike was called, which was much harder for the government to deal with than different local strikes. It was also difficult for the NUM because (a) not all miners thought their jobs were under threat and (b) many miners were unhappy that there had not been a national ballot.
- The strike was called without a national ballot: this meant there was no delay and ensured that the strike went ahead – previous ballots for strike action against pit closure plans had seen some miners voting not to strike.
- The strike was set out as a fight for survival against a government determined to destroy miners and the unions. This was a powerful call to action, but also set up the protest as all or nothing: there was little room for compromise or negotiation.
- 'Flying pickets' were used: because miners in some 'economic' mines (especially in Nottinghamshire) didn't want to strike, pickets were transported to these pits from supportive areas.
- The media was used to describe police intimidation and brutality against miners.
- The solidarity and pride of miners' communities was drawn on to keep the strike going despite economic hardship.
- Women in mining communities played a huge role in supporting the strike, organising marches, raising funds and supporting struggling families.
- The NUM only gave financial support to miners who were picketing strikers; other miners did not get support. This put pressure on all miners who weren't working to join the strike.
- Miners who didn't strike were called 'scabs' and were ostracised in many mining communities. There was great intimidation and some violence against scabs.
- Picketing miners resisted police attempts to get workers across the picket line; fights between police and miners happened. It was a bitter, violent protest. Calls for support went out to other unions. However, many UK unions did not support the strike because of the lack of a national ballot and because it was seen as the wrong kind of union action – an all-out fight rather than a negotiated process.
- Posters, badges and leaflets were distributed to give information and raise much-needed funds. The NUM also successfully appealed for money and food from trade unionists abroad.
- Links were made to other groups who opposed the Conservatives' politics and there was a lot of support from popular culture.

The miners' tactics

The government's tactics

- Between 1979 and 1984, the Conservative government passed several laws reducing trade union rights.
- The Thatcher government had stockpiled coal, converted some power stations from coal to oil and recruited private hauliers to transport coal in case railway workers went out on strike too. This meant that power stations kept on producing energy throughout the strike.
- When the NUM called a national strike without a ballot first according to the new laws, the government was able to use legal powers to fine the NUM; when the NUM refused to pay up, the courts seized NUM assets – £5 million. This meant that the NUM had much less money to help support striking miners.
- The lack of a national ballot also meant that the government could call the strike illegal and say that strikers were acting as a mob, rather than following democratic procedures.
- Because the strike was ruled illegal, the government refused to pay state benefits to many miners, forcing them and their families into real poverty. This put huge pressure on miners to break the strike.
  - Divide and conquer – the government promised the miners of Nottinghamshire that their pits were economic and their jobs were safe.
  - Many other unions were unhappy about the lack of a ballot and didn't support the strike. The government got information about NUM plans from sources in other unions.
- The government brought in police from all over the country to build up a massive police presence in strike areas. The view was also that local police might be too sympathetic to the miners.
- Police were also used to prevent strikers (the 'flying pickets') from travelling between strike areas – for example, by using road blocks.
- The government fed the media with information about alleged corruption in the NUM, including stories that the NUM had accepted funds from the Soviet Union. Even MI5 were used.
- Government media appearances continually stressed that strikers used violent intimidation against miners who wanted to work.

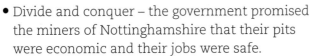

The government's tactics

Source D: Comments made by Prime Minister Margaret Thatcher to the government minister in charge of Energy, Peter Walker, in 1983.

> Almost certainly in this Parliament we'll have an attempt by Scargill to have a major strike. He tried three times in the last government and I'm sure he'll keep on trying. I want you to handle it.

Source E: Part of a report about an alleged incident, which appeared in the *Sun* newspaper on 9 May 1984.

Miners 'firing ball bearings'

PICKET bullies fired ball bearings yesterday at Notts pitmen defying the walkout call by miners' leader Arthur Scargill.

The frustrated strikers used catapults to shoot the metal balls at vehicles carrying the rebels into Pye Hill pit near Nottingham. Several windows were smashed.

The plucky drivers still took most of the workers through for the afternoon shift.

Scargill . . . walkout call defied

Activities

1 Using the sources and information in this topic, describe how you think the government had learned lessons from its failure to cope with the successful strikes of the early 1970s.

2 Identify possible strengths and weaknesses in the tactics of both sides. Which side do you think had the most power?

Summary

- Miners' leaders decided on regional ballots, rather than a national one, and used flying pickets.
- The government had prepared well for this strike, reducing trade union rights by altering industrial relations laws, stockpiling coal and using the benefits system, the courts and the police to undermine the strike.

8.3 The miners' strike: reporting 'The Battle of Orgreave'

Learning outcomes

By the end of this topic you should be able to:

- describe media coverage of the violence in the miners' strike
- identify possible biases in media sources from the period.

Source A: Selected results of Gallup opinion polls held during the strike.

Question 1	Where do your sympathies lie?			
	Employers	Miners	Neither	Don't know
July 1984	40%	33%	19%	8%
December 1984	51%	26%	18%	5%

Question 2	Do you approve/disapprove of the methods used by the miners?		
	Approve	Disapprove	Don't know
July 1984	15%	79%	6%
December 1984	7%	88%	5%

Question 3	Are the miners using responsible or irresponsible methods?		
	Responsible	Irresponsible	Don't know
July 1984	12%	78%	10%
December 1984	9%	84%	7%

The media and public opinion

Public opinion during the strike was divided and varied greatly in different regions. While the strike was on, public opinion in the Home Counties (except Kent) was mixed, whereas in the Welsh valleys, Yorkshire and other areas actually affected by the strike, support was high. Overall, however, the government generally had more support than the miners.

Newspapers such as the *Sun* and the *Daily Mail* took a very anti-strike position from the start of the strike, and even the *Daily Mirror* became increasingly hostile as the strike went on. Only left-wing newspapers such as the *Morning Star* and *Socialist Worker* were constantly supportive of the striking miners.

At the time, NUM members claimed that most of the media seemed determined to show violent scenes of conflict, even though they claimed it was mostly between relatively unarmed men and some women who were facing large numbers of well-organised police armed with truncheons, riot shields and horses. Public support for miners was badly affected by scenes of 'mobs' of miners attacking police and 'scabs'.

'The Battle of Orgreave'

Some of the most publicised scenes showed violence between police and miners' pickets on 18 June 1984 outside the Orgreave Coking Plant in South Yorkshire. Television coverage showed strikers hurling rocks, bricks and bottles at the police who, after much provocation, finally retaliated with a mass charge on the pickets. This coverage badly affected public support for the miners. Many union leaders and Labour members criticised the strikers' behaviour. The media increasingly attacked the miners and the strike. NUM area leaders then decided to call off further mass pickets. Within days, the amount of coke taken out of Orgreave increased dramatically.

Mistakes or manipulation?

The BBC later admitted that the order of events had been reversed. The actual film footage shows that the mounted police attacked a peaceful picket line first and inflicted serious injuries upon several pickets, with the miners only then fighting back, not the other way round.

It is now widely agreed that the police seriously overreacted to the situation at Orgreave. As well as police in riot gear, mounted police also charged the picket lines. For the first time, the number of injured pickets was double that of injured police.

Source B: An extract from part of the text of the letter of apology issued by the BBC on 3 July 1991, six years after the end of the strike.

'The BBC acknowledged some years ago that it made a mistake over our sequence of events at Orgreave. We accepted without question that it was serious, but emphasized that it was a mistake made in the haste of putting the news together. … The end result was that the editor inadvertently reversed the occurrence of the actions of the police and the pickets.'

Activities

1. How might Source B help to understand the figures provided in Source A?

2. What other aspects of the strike might also explain those figures?

Source C: Lesley Boulton, a member of Sheffield's Women's Support Group, trying to call an ambulance for an injured picketer at Orgreave, 18 June 1984.

Source D: Picketing miners: goading the police at Orgreave or protesting against police violence?

Summary

- Most of the media did not support the strike.
- Violence against non-strikers and the police reduced public support for the strike.
- Miners complained that the media focused on violent incidents and manipulated the news against the strike.

ResultsPlus
Build better answers

Study Source A on page 134, Source C on page 132 and Source E on page 133.

Do you think the media coverage was the main reason that the miners' strike was defeated? Explain your answer, using your own knowledge, Sources A, C and E and any other sources on pages 132–135 which you find helpful. (16 marks)

■ **Basic, Level 1 (1–4 marks)**
Answer makes valid comments but without detail from the sources, for example 'the media turned people against the miners'.

● **Good, Level 2 (5–8 marks)**
Answer supports comments with details from the sources. For example, the answer may mention that the language used in Source E is very biased against the miners, calling them 'bullies', and Source A shows that the reporting of Orgreave turned people against the miners. Answers that also add detail from the student's own knowledge will get higher marks in the level.

▲ **Better, Level 3 (9–13 marks)**
Answer deals thoroughly with the impact of media coverage using at least three sources, and will also add other factors, e.g. the police strength demonstrated in Source C. Answers that also add detail from the student's own knowledge will get higher marks in the level.

▲ **Excellent, Level 4 (14–16 marks)**
In addition to the above, the answer also shows the importance of other factors, e.g. the government's organisation and use of the law and the courts. The answer will then reach a balanced judgment using sources and own knowledge.

8.4 The miners' strike: supporting the strike

Learning outcomes

By the end of this topic you should be able to:

- describe the role of women in the miners' strike
- describe how mining communities tried to cope with growing financial hardships.

The financial costs of striking

September 1984 was a turning point in the miners' strike. The High Court ruled that the NUM had breached its own constitution by calling a strike without first holding a national ballot. As a result of this decision:

- striking miners were not entitled to state benefits, which forced the majority of miners and their families to survive the strike on handouts and charity
- the NUM was fined and refused to pay, resulting in the courts seizing NUM funds: South Wales NUM was fined £50,000, for example, and then had £770,000 of funds seized by the courts when it refused to pay up. This reduced the ability of the NUM to support strikers.

Poverty and hunger became rife in the mining heartlands. Many miners faced the same dilemma:

to return to work and be viewed as a 'scab', or to remain on strike and be unable to provide for their families.

To help them survive, a wide network of miners' support groups was set up. These were often led by miners' wives and girlfriends. On 11 August, the Women Against Pit Closures organisation held its first demonstration in London. Support groups organised thousands of collections outside supermarkets, set up communal kitchens and organised benefit concerts, all in an attempt to help the miners to win the strike.

The role of women in the strike

Traditionally, mining and mining communities had been very male-dominated. Women had had no active role in strikes. Now, however, large numbers of women began to take action and develop growing independence, well beyond the usual 'women's work' of providing food and drink. As well as setting up soup kitchens (last seen in mining areas during the General Strike), women supported the picket lines, organised meetings and travelled across the country to speak at fund-raising meetings. Particularly important were the Women Against Pit Closures and the various Women's Support Groups.

Source A: The National Women's Rally, 12 May 1984, organised by British Women Against Pit Closures.

Union support – why didn't other unions support the strike?

Although the TUC voted on 3 September 1984 to support the miners, nothing really came of this and some unions refused to support the miners. These included the Electrical, Electronic, Telecommunications and Plumbing Union (EETPU), and the Steelworkers' Union, despite the fact that in the steel strike of 1980 miners had supported them. The Labour Party also did not support the strike due to the lack of a paper ballot, although several local Labour Party branches raised funds to support striking miners and their families. If the unions were to be effective in a democracy, they had to represent all their members.

Source B: Women's Support Groups and miners marching to a rally at Cowden Park, 25 August 1984.

Source C: Part of the Women Against Pit Closures' campaign song.

> We are women, we are strong,
> We are fighting for our lives
> Side by side with our men
> Who work the nation's mines,
> United by the struggle,
> United by the past,
> And it's – Here we go! Here we go!
> For the women of the working class.

On 28 September, the National Association of Colliery Overmen, Deputies and Shotfirers (NACODS) voted to go on strike and, on 17 October, called for a strike for 25 October. In the end, however, they called it off. The government and the Coal Board had convinced them that a strike was not in their best interests.

At the same time, the National Coal Board (NCB) began to offer special cash payments, bonuses and increased wages to striking miners who returned to work before the end of the month. Miners were also encouraged to go back to work with the promise that if they did and later accepted redundancy, they would get £1,000 for every year they had worked in the industry. The numbers of miners drifting back to work began to increase.

Activities

For discussion

3 Should the other unions have supported the miners in this strike? Would the outcome of the strike have been different if they had?

Activities

Study Sources A, B and C.

1 What do these three sources suggest about the role of women during the miners' strike?

2 Do they provide sufficient evidence to conclude that women played an important role in keeping the strike going? Use the sources and the information in this lesson to explain your answer.

Summary

- The role of women in the miners' strike was much more significant than in previous miners' strikes and helped to keep the strike going.

- The decision of the NUM not to hold a ballot before the national strike was called helped to prevent other unions from joining the strike.

8.5 The miners' strike: outcomes

Learning outcomes

By the end of this topic you should be able to:

- give reasons why the strike ended in failure for the NUM
- describe how miners reacted when the strike was officially ended.

Fading support for the miners

Support for the miners began to fade following the manslaughter of a taxi driver driving a working miner to work in South Wales on 1 December. Then, on 5 December, Ian MacGregor announced plans to privatise some pits. On 14 December, the TUC began to put pressure on the NUM to settle. On 7 January 1985, the NCB claimed that 1,200 striking miners had returned to work, although these figures were disputed by the NUM leaders.

Source A: A protest outside Seafield Colliery, Scotland, as a bus carrying 'drift backs' arrives.

More talks between the NCB and the NUM in February also failed and, on 13 February, the High Court banned all mass picketing in Yorkshire. The Yorkshire NUM was faced with an injunction that pickets should not have more than six miners.

Source B: Comments made by a miner's wife on a picket at Yorkshire Main Colliery.

> If the men can't or won't picket because of the injunction then it's up to us women to show them the way. We don't belong to the NUM – there's nothing they can do to us.

Source C: Members of a Women's Support Group picketing Yorkshire Main Colliery, 21 February 1985.

Activities

Study Sources A, B and C.

1. What can you learn about the determination of men and women in mining areas in late 1984/ early 1985 to continue the strike?
2. How useful are these sources as evidence of support for the strike?
3. What tactics did the authorities use to weaken the strike?

If this was broken, then area funds would be confiscated by the courts – again showing the government's ability to use their new laws to put pressure on the strike.

On 28 February, Ian MacGregor announced that sacked miners would not be re-employed. On 2 March, a meeting of Yorkshire miners voted to continue the strike, but the following day the NUM, despite pleas by Arthur Scargill, voted 98 to 91 for a return to work. The NUM ended the strike without gaining any concessions from the NCB.

After 51 weeks of struggle, the strike had officially come to an end. However, unlike the General Strike of 1926, when miners had stayed locked out for six months before returning to work, returning miners decided to celebrate their year-long struggle. They went back to work with heads held high, and with brass bands playing and banners flying. In several pits, on the day the miners went back, Miners' Wives Support Groups gathered at the colliery gates to give carnations to the returning miners – the flower is seen as something to be given to heroes.

Source D: Miners from Armthorpe Colliery marching back to work, 8 March 1985.

Source E: Comments made by Lynne Cheetham about the return to work of miners at the Point of Ayr Colliery, North Wales.

We walk with our heads up. The scabs look at their boots. It wasn't the sort of victory we might have won, but we went through the year with dignity.

Activities

4   What strengths enabled the strike to last so long?

5   What tactics were the authorities able to use to weaken the strike in the end?

For discussion

6   Do you think the strike should have been fought?

  Do you think a national ballot should have been held before a national strike was called?

  Just before the strike, the government had been certain it would be defeated in a few weeks. Why do you think it was so confident and what factors proved it wrong?

The aftermath of the strike

The end of the strike was felt as a terrible blow by many NUM members, although they largely understood that the extreme poverty that families had suffered as a result of no wages and reduced state benefits for a year meant they could no longer continue. In many areas, striking miners had different attitudes from those who had returned to work after being on strike for only a couple of months, compared to those who felt forced to return to work for the sake of their children, many months later.

Many NUM members strongly condemned the Nottinghamshire branch as strike-breakers. Despite Conservative government promises made to keep Nottinghamshire pits open, most of these were closed too in the years from 1985 to 1994.

Summary

- Fading public support, government pressure and economic hardship forced the eventual end of the strike.

- The impact of the strike affected communities for many years.

- The government continued a programme of pit closures – even those that had been 'economic' in the 1980s.

8.6 Source enquiry skills: the usefulness of sources

Learning outcomes

By the end of this topic you should be able to:

- show understanding that the usefulness of a source varies depending on the enquiry
- understand how the usefulness of a source should be evaluated
- evaluate a source's usefulness.

Value of the source

To evaluate the usefulness of a source properly, you should think about what makes its information valuable for your enquiry. Consider the following.

Relevance

What sort of information does the source give and how much does it apply to your enquiry?

Strength

Does the evidence have any added strength because of its origins, nature or purpose?

Types of sources

An event like the one in this picture will produce a range of sources:

- Police reports
- Newspaper reports
- TV footage
- Medical reports
- Private letters
- Court reports

ResultsPlus
Watch out!

Many students think the usefulness of a source depends only on how much information it contains.

Useful information

The usefulness of a source varies according to what the historian is investigating. A diary entry from Arthur Scargill might be very helpful if the historian wants to know how the strike was organised, but it will be less useful for finding out about the impact of the strike on miners' families. For the historian, a miner's account and a police officer's account of the 'Battle of Orgreave' (pages 134–135) might be equally useful but in different ways.

When evaluating a source's usefulness, you need always to have in your mind the words 'useful for what?'. This will help you to be clearer about how the information in the source relates to your enquiry.

When an important event occurs, such as a large protest, it will create a range of historical sources.

To evaluate a source, keep the focus of the enquiry in your mind. For example, is the photograph in the diagram below useful for any of these enquiries? It shows miners marching back to work on 8 March 1985.

How well was the protest led?	What tactics were used by protesters?	How successful were the tactics used by the government?

What role did the media play?	Why did the strike end?	How did miners feel about it?

Activities

1 Think about giving plus and minus points to evaluate the source.

Look at the photograph at the bottom right of page 140. What are its strengths and weaknesses if you want to use it to find out why the strike ended? Copy and complete the table below – the first line has been filled in for you.

Plus points	Minus points
The photograph shows a mass return to work, with a large number of supporters. The union banner suggests the miners remained proud of their struggle.	It is only one photograph and gives no information about why the strike ended, just provides a sense of the emotions involved.

ResultsPlus
Watch out!

Don't assume that a source must be reliable to be useful. Unreliable sources can still be useful, so you need to weigh up the strengths and limitations of each source according to what you want to find out.

Source A: From a speech by the Prime Minster, Margaret Thatcher, on 30 May 1984, the day after the first mass picket at Orgreave.

I must tell you that what we have got is an attempt to substitute the rule of the mob for the rule of law. It must not succeed. They are using violence and intimidation to impose their will on others who do not want it… The rule of law must prevail over the rule of the mob.

Source B: Pickets at Orgreave running from a police charge, 18 June 1984.

Evaluating usefulness

Sources A and B are both about the events at Orgreave (see pages 134–135). They are useful in different ways.

Source A is useful for finding out what the Prime Minister thought about the events. It is strong evidence about her attitudes, but it is weak evidence if you want to find out what actually happened. She talks about the 'rule of the mob' and 'violence and intimidation', but you would need to check that.

Source B is more useful than Source A for finding out about an actual event at Orgreave. It is strong evidence of forceful police action at Orgreave, but what are its weaknesses? Because it captures only a moment in time, you do not know what happened before this. Were the strikers behaving like a mob at Orgreave as the Prime Minister said in Source A? Remember, too, that she was talking about 29 May and this date is different.

Activities

2 Study Sources A and B.

How useful are the sources for a historian trying to find out how much violence there was at Orgreave in 1984?

ResultsPlus
Top tip!

The examiner is not looking for a 'right answer' to this question. You only need to show that you have thought about the relevance and the strength of the evidence.

Summary

- Sources are useful in different ways, depending on the focus of the historian's enquiry. All sources should be evaluated according to what you want to find out.
- The strength of the evidence is affected by its nature, origin and purpose.

9.1 The poll tax protests: introduction of the poll tax

Learning outcomes

By the end of this topic you will be able to:

- find out about the poll tax and what it meant
- discover how people reacted to it.

What was the poll tax?

By 1990, the Conservative government wanted to change the way that local government was financed. The plan was to replace the existing rates system with a community charge, or 'poll tax', as it came to be called. This would be a tax on everyone over 18, with every person paying the same amount.

The old rates system was based on an estimate of the value of each house, so people with expensive houses paid more than people with poor houses. It didn't matter if lots of people or one person lived there, the rate was the same. The money from rates went to fund local governments. Large numbers of people paid nothing towards the local services they used. Under the new system, all adults in a family would pay, but it also meant that very wealthy people and poor people would be paying the same amount.

Source A: Nicholas Ridley, the Conservative Environment Secretary, 1 April 1988. Ridley was responsible for implementing the poll tax.

Why should a duke pay more than a dustman? It is only because we have been subjected to socialist ideas for the last 50 years that people think this is fair.

In 1987, a law was passed to introduce the new tax in Scotland on 1 April 1989. It was then to apply to the rest of Britain (with the exception of Northern Ireland) from 1 April 1990.

It was a flat rate tax, and took no account of a person's ability to pay, unless they were in the very poorest income categories.

All those over 18 were liable (except the homeless, the 'severely mentally impaired' and members of religious communities).

The act also set up a register of all those over 18 who were liable for the new tax.

Source B: An extract from the *Guardian* newspaper, 1989. The Duke of Westminster was and still is one of the wealthiest men in Britain.

The Duke of Westminster, who used to pay £10,255 in rates on his estate has just learned his new Poll tax: £417. His house-keeper and resident chauffeur face precisely the same bill.

Early reactions

As soon as these changes were announced and the details emerged, opposition began and became increasingly widespread. Several surveys showed that more than 70 per cent of the population would be considerably worse off as a result of the introduction of the poll tax. Even those on income support had to pay at least 20 per cent of the tax. Those living in private rented accommodation were particularly hard hit, as many landlords did not reduce their rents, which had included an element for the rates under the old system. It was estimated that by January 1990, Scottish landlords had made about £40 million in this way, while *The Observer* in August 1990 estimated that in England and Wales private landlords would make over £100 million.

Activities

Study Sources A and B.

1 What does Source A tell you about the justification for the poll tax?

2 What does Source B tell you about why the new tax was immediately very unpopular?

Protest or resistance?

In Scotland, where the poll tax was first introduced, public opinion was divided on how to react. The Labour Party and the trade unions argued for traditional protest marches and campaigns within the law to persuade the government to drop the tax. In the run-up to the new tax, they organised a 'Scottish Campaign Against the Poll Tax', and many leaflets, stickers and posters were printed. Other groups also organised events, letter-writing and information campaigns.

However, many local grass-roots communities in Scotland decided that more needed to be done. As well as organising protest marches and demonstrations, they also called for the establishment of a network of local groups opposed to the tax. Most importantly, they also decided to resist the new tax.

This set up an important divide in the tactics of opposition to the poll tax:

- protest within the law: campaigns to build public opposition to the point at which it would vote out the Conservatives
- resistance to the law: people prepared to disobey the law and take the consequences.

The four main methods of resistance

- non-registration – and ignoring the fines imposed as a result of non-registration
- non-payment – but not as individuals; instead, this should be done via organised local groups that would defend all those taken to court
- non-implementation – i.e. calling on councils to refuse to administer the tax
- non-collection – asking all union-members responsible for collection to refuse to do it.

Source C: An early poll tax resister.

Summary

- The Conservative Party introduced the community charge (poll tax) as part of their drive to make everyone contribute to local taxes.
- The poll tax was immediately unpopular because most people would be worse off.
- Opposition to the poll tax included both lawful protest and resistance (i.e. refusal to obey the law).

Activities

3 Which of these methods of resistance do you think would be most effective?

4 What role could organisations play to support resistance?

9.2 The poll tax protests: grass-roots organisation and tactics

Learning outcomes

By the end of this topic you will be able to:

- examine tactics of resistance to the poll tax
- discover how opposition was organised
- consider the impact of these forms of protest.

Non-payment

The most significant form of resistance was non-payment of the poll tax. People not registering as they were supposed to was also important, but the numbers involved in non-payment were huge.

- By September 1989, at least 15 per cent of Scots were not paying the tax (remember it was introduced in Scotland in April 1989).
- By April 1990, official figures for Scotland showed that nearly 1 million people had not paid a penny of this new tax.
- The tax became law in England in April 1990. By July 1990, there were 14 million non-payers, 97,000 in the London borough of Haringey alone (Haringey was a Labour authority and a leading area of resistance to the tax).
- By January 1991 in England, non-payment averaged 18 per cent in rural areas, 27 per cent in most major urban areas and 34 per cent in inner London.
- By January 1991 in Scotland, non-payment was nearly 35 per cent.
- By March 1991, over 18 million people were refusing to pay the poll tax.
- Once the abolition of the poll tax was announced, non-payment levels went up to over 50 per cent in many London boroughs, and places such as Bristol and Strathclyde.

When the poll tax ended in 1993, it was estimated that £2.5 billion of the tax was still unpaid.

Source A: Protesters in Brighton burning poll tax bills in 1989. Scenes like this took place in many areas across Britain.

Source B: Comments made by Kenny MacAskill, Vice Chair of the Scottish National Party, in *The Scotsman*, 12 January 1988.

> If 100,000 Scots are prepared to say no to paying the poll tax, that is going to put unbearable pressure on the Tories' position in Scotland. Our judgement is that would be enough to make the government back down.

Activities

1 Study Sources A and B. Do they support the view that non-payment was a protest, or just a case of many people not being able to afford to pay?

Organisation

Non-payment caused huge problems for the government: it couldn't arrest 18 million people. It was difficult to suggest that this was simple criminal behaviour, when those refusing to pay made it clear that they were doing so as a protest. When people were taken to court for non-payment, they often then refused to pay their fine (only 28 per cent of those taken to court paid up in England and Wales); some even went to prison in protest.

Also, this wasn't a protest organised by the Labour Party or the trade unions, neither of whom were comfortable with encouraging people to break the law. The government didn't have the traditional set-up for negotiations. The protest was organised in a new way – by local groups, which became called Anti-Poll Tax Unions (APTUs).

The first of these APTUs was set up in Maryhill, Glasgow, in April 1987. By January 1988, it had over 2,000 members. This sparked off a large number of similar groups, first in Edinburgh and then all over Scotland. Organisers in Scotland sent information and speakers to groups in England and Wales. By November 1989, there were over 1,000 local Anti-Poll Tax Unions in England and Wales. Many of these community-based groups then linked up to form regional federations.

What did APTUs do?

As it was such a local-based campaign, there were many different approaches and tactics, but in essence the APTUs gave out information and supported those not registering or not paying the poll tax. For instance, the Haringey Anti-Poll Tax Union and the Tottenham Against the Poll Tax Organisation:

- produced a series of leaflets giving information about non-payment and how to avoid bailiffs seizing goods
- flyposted handmade posters and spray painted on walls to publicise resistance
- made T-shirts, badges and mugs with anti-poll tax slogans.

Posters were often written out by hand with felt tip pens, photocopied and then flyposted on walls.

When councils tried to send in bailiffs to seize the goods of non-payers, local APTU groups often organised protests that prevented their entry. If anyone appeared in court, the local APTUs not only organised demonstrations, but also provided legal advice, which often led to cases being suspended. Despite the scale of non-payment, only 120 people were ever imprisoned for it.

Source C: Comments made by Chris Moyers of the Mayfield APTU in Midlothian, Scotland, showing the desire at local level for a loose-based organisation. Sheriff officers in Scotland performed the same role as bailiffs in England and Wales.

> We had one member who was very officious and wanted everything done right. We couldn't quite see the point. We just wanted to get out there and fight against sheriff officers.

Source D: A handbill produced by the Broughton/Inverleith Anti-Poll Tax Group in Scotland in July 1990, telling non-tax payers how to deal with threatening letters from the council.

23 JULY 1990
POLL TAX UPDATE

The Council have sent out a batch of new warning letters about Poll Tax arrears.

The letters will say that " a Summary Warrant has been granted against you" and gives you 5 days to pay. What this means is that the matter is now in the hands of the Sheriff Officers.

IGNORE THEM

These letters are nothing more than a threat . 150,000 people got these same letters in December or March and nothing has happened to them.

If you are still worried, or have recieved a different letter then you should contact the Anti Poll Tax Group for advice The group meets every Wednesday in Drummond Community High at 7:30 pm. ALL WELCOME.

LOCAL CONTACTS-

Broughton Inverleith Anti Poll Tax Group

Activities

Study Sources C and D.

2 What can you learn about the Anti-Poll Tax Union campaigns from these sources?

3 Why might such organisations make it difficult for the authorities to take action against leading campaigners?

Summary

- The scale of non-payment meant that it was impossible for the government to deal with.
- Non-payment was supported and promoted by local organisations, not through any central organisation, which the government could try to weaken.

145

9.3 The poll tax protests: the Battle of Trafalgar Square, 31 March 1990

Learning outcomes

By the end of this topic you should be able to:

- find out about some of those involved in the leadership of the campaign against the poll tax
- evaluate the events of 31 March 1990.

The All-Britain Anti Poll Tax Federation (ABAPTF)

As the movement grew, with APTUs linking up to form regional federations, an All-Britain Federation was set up (in 1989) to organise a more national campaign. At first, the All-Britain Federation organised a series of regional protest demonstrations to take place just before the poll tax was implemented in England and Wales.

In the South West alone, over 50,000 people took part in local demonstrations in places such as Plymouth, Exeter, Bristol, Bath and Stroud. Wherever local councils met to set the rate of the new poll tax, protests took place. Some were peaceful; others, like the one in Bristol, saw clashes between protesters and police.

As well as organising local and regional demonstrations, the All-Britain Federation decided to hold a national demonstration in London on 31 March 1990.

Leadership

Unlike the other protests covered in this topic, the campaign against the poll tax did not have many prominent national leaders. The All-Britain Federation grew out of the local organisations, rather than leading them, and its leaders represented lots of different interest groups, including left-wing parties like the Militant Tendency, the Socialist Workers Party, members of APTU federations and even extreme left-wing anarchist groups. There was inevitably some

disagreement about strategy between all these different groups. Most organisation and support continued to be at the local level.

The events of 31 March 1990

When the All-Britain Federation called for a national demonstration at Trafalgar Square in London on 31 March 1990, their organisers had no idea that as many as 200,000 protesters would turn up on the day: they were expecting 20,000. Trafalgar Square only had capacity for 60,000. However, the police refused a request to change the venue.

Source A: Some of the crowd who demonstrated in London against the poll tax on 31 March 1990.

Activities

1 Study Source A. What can you learn about the demonstrators from looking at this source?

The first violence

Initially, there was low-profile policing, and the crowd, a mixture of young people, families with their children and old-age pensioners, was good-natured. Then, about 20 protesters staged a sit-down outside Downing Street, after they had been refused permission to hand in a petition at Number 10. A small minority then tried to get over the barricades at the end of Downing Street. Demonstrators later claimed that the police deliberately provoked the demonstrators.

Source B: An extract from the Trafalgar Square Defendants' Campaign's legal meeting minutes, 27 May 1990.

> A man in a wheelchair was attacked and arrested by the police, separated from his wheelchair and thrown into a police van. A woman was arrested and, in front of the crowd, stripped of her clothes. Both arrests angered and incensed the crowd. It was an obvious police provocation of a peaceful demonstration.

Another 300 people then decided to sit down in protest. Increasingly violent clashes began between police and a minority of the demonstrators, mainly anarchists (from groups such as Class War) and supporters of far-left groups such as the Militant Tendency and the Socialist Workers Party.

From violence to riot

When mounted riot police baton-charged the crowd, bottles, rocks and sticks were thrown at the police. As the rest of the crowd moved away, about 3,000 demonstrators remained and a major riot broke out, which spread to much of the West End: cars were damaged, shop windows were smashed and shops were looted.

Source C: A protester kicks the window of a fast-food store in Lower Regent Street.

By the end of the day, 341 people had been arrested and 542 police officers had been injured. There were no official records of demonstrators injured, but some put the figure into thousands, some of them ordinary people who simply got in the way of the police who thought they were demonstrators.

Source D: Comments by Tommy Sheridan, the Chair of the All-Britain Federation, at a press conference called immediately after the march.

> The majority of those who became embroiled in the running battles had nothing to do with our protest.

Source E: A photograph of police in riot gear clashing with protesters in Trafalgar Square, during the riot of 31 March 1990.

Activities

Study Sources A–E in this topic.

2 What do the sources suggest about the policing of the demonstration?

3 Would you expect these events to increase support for the poll tax protest or for the government?

4 Source D says that the violence had nothing to do with the official poll tax protest. If so, was the lack of central organisation of the protest a weakness in the campaign?

Summary

- Although different groups claimed leadership of the poll tax protests, there was no overall control.
- The police response to the demonstration on 31 March 1990 aggravated tensions.
- A minority of demonstrators were responsible for the rioting.

9.4 The poll tax protests: the end of the poll tax

Learning outcomes

By the end of this topic you should be able to:

- explain what anti-poll tax campaigners did after the march and riot of 31 March 1990
- describe how the poll tax was finally replaced by the Conservative government
- find out about the attitudes of the media to the anti-poll tax campaign.

The poll tax and Thatcher's fall

While the non-payment protest had been impossible for the government to tackle, the riot of 31 March 1990 was more like the 'traditional' protest the authorities were trained for. However, the heavy-handed policing and the images of rioting in the West End of London suggested instead that the government had no control over events. 'Hot-headed' frontline police officers were blamed for 'isolated incidents' of 'gratuitous violence'. The march and riot were widely reported by the foreign press, many asking whether this was the end of 'Thatcherism'.

On the other side of the protest, there were fears that the riot might lead to a loss of public support (as was seen following violence in the miners' strike). In fact, the campaign grew in strength, and protests against the poll tax continued all over the country.

Conservative Party MPs became concerned about their growing unpopularity, especially when they began to do badly in the local elections in May 1990. Thatcher had personally championed the poll tax and was so strongly associated with what it stood for that she was eventually forced to resign as Prime Minister by Conservative leaders in November 1990.

The end of the poll tax

A week later, Margaret Thatcher was replaced by John Major. After some debate over whether the poll tax could be reformed, the new Prime Minister finally announced (in April 1991) that it would be replaced by a new council tax. However, until then, the poll tax would continue as the new tax would not begin until April 1993. As a result, the protests continued too.

Source A: A poster depicting the new Conservative Prime Minister, John Major, and advertising the 23 March 1991 anti-poll tax demonstration.

The role of the media

At first, the media generally tended just to report the refusal of resisters to pay the tax, and the various local campaigns and demonstrations against it. This was certainly true of many local papers. As the organisation of the campaign had few national figures, it was difficult to identify and attack individuals.

However, in March 1990 when local demonstrations outside town halls against the setting of the poll tax by councils resulted in clashes between protesters and the police, many newspapers condemned what were often described as 'rent-a-mob' extremists from political groups such as Militant Tendency and the Socialist Workers Party.

Source B: An extract from an article in the *Evening Standard*, 5 April 1990.

FRONT-LINE VICTIMS OF THE POLL TAX WAR

Council Poll tax inspectors are now bearing the brunt of the public's fury over the community charge. ... And every day, the men and women at the sharp end of the tax have to venture into "hostile" territory.

The most alarming... include...

Buckets of urine being thrown from balconies on Broadwater Farm as a group of officers... tried to deliver registration forms.

In Camden, canvassers have had abuse shouted at them and in the neighbouring borough of Islington, officers have been threatened with dogs and pelted with eggs.

Most newspapers also strongly criticised actions taken against the council officers who tried to collect registration forms or bailiffs trying to collect payments or seize goods for non-payment.

After the riots on 31 March 1990, many of the national newspapers took a strong line against those involved. Many, such as the *Sun* and the

People, printed photographs taken by the police of demonstrators they wanted to question, and asked their readers to give the names of those they recognised to the police. Nonetheless, television footage was broadcast, some of which seemed to show demonstrators being deliberately hit by police vans or trampled by horses.

Source D: Comments made on 2 June 1990 by Norman Tebbit, then the Chair of the Conservative Party.

If you tell people to break the law by not paying the tax, you're not far off telling them to break other laws as well.

Source C: Pages from The *People* newspaper, 13 May 1990, following the 31 March anti-poll tax demonstration in London.

Activities

Study Sources A–C.

1 Do these show that the media were biased against the poll tax resisters or against violent tactics? Explain your answer.

2 The term 'rent-a-mob' often occurred in media coverage of the 31 March demonstration. What does this phrase suggest about the way the media viewed the protest as a whole?

3 Study Source D. What can you infer from this source about how some Conservatives viewed the protest as a whole?

For discussion

4 The poll tax protesters defeated the Thatcher government while the miners' strike was beaten by it. What were the differences between the two protests that might explain this? Consider causes, leaders, tactics and the response of the authorities.

Summary

- The poll tax protest led to the tax being abolished and, indirectly, caused Margaret Thatcher to be forced to resign.

- Mass non-payment was a very successful tactic, but whether the tactic was organised or spontaneous (or a mixture of both) is debatable.

9.5 Source enquiry skills: making a judgement

Learning outcomes

By the end of this topic you should be able to:

- analyse questions and plan an answer
- use the sources and your own knowledge
- reach a judgement after weighing the evidence.

The final question in the examination asks you to use sources and knowledge to make a judgement on an issue about protest in this period. You may be asked why something happened or how important it was, or to evaluate the role of factors in protest.

To gain the best marks

- Remember that in history there is rarely a clear-cut answer; usually you have to weigh up two sides of an issue.
- Plan your answer so that you build up a logical argument rather than produce random comments.

- make sure that each of your comments is supported by points from the sources in the examination paper and/or from your own knowledge.

Study the following example

'The poll tax was defeated mainly by passive resistance.'

How far do you agree with this statement? Explain your answer, using Sources A, B and C and your own knowledge.

Start by analysing the questions

- What topic knowledge do you need? Facts about the poll tax and its end.
- What does the question want you to do? Explain the factors involved in why the poll tax ended and show which was the most important.
- How do you do it?
  (i) identify factors from the sources and your own knowledge.
  (ii) show the effect of each factor and make a judgement about their importance.
- Look at the sources. How can you use them?

Source A: Part of an anti-poll tax demonstration, 27 May 1990. The 'figure' to be burnt represents the Conservative Prime Minister, Margaret Thatcher.

The demonstration suggests that PEACEFUL PROTEST was a factor

The printed posters suggest that ORGANISATION was a factor

These show the importance of PUBLIC OPINION, since the government needed the support of voters to be re-elected.

Source B: From an article in *The Observer* newspaper, 24 March 1991.

> The poll tax was killed by non-payment. This weekend each and every one of those non-payers should feel proud of themselves… The alliance between the poor and the prosperous in the effort to sabotage an immoral law proved that such a thing could be done. It was left to a rag-tag army of ordinary people to destroy a bad law.

This suggests that PASSIVE RESISTANCE was the key factor.

The author says that ordinary people have destroyed the poll tax, killed by non-payment.

Source C: From *Britain 1945–2007* written by Michael Lynch, 2008.

> Opposition [to the poll tax] was immediate and **organised**. Millions of people refused or avoided payment. Even the respectable middle classes, **previously** Margaret Thatcher's strongest allies, began to protest. The most serious disturbance came with a **violent anti-poll tax demonstration** in London's Trafalgar Square on 31 March.

Suggests Margaret Thatcher was losing voter support and that PUBLIC OPINION was a factor influencing the government.

Suggests the use of VIOLENT PROTEST was a factor.

Suggests ORGANISATION was a factor.

Now think about your own knowledge. What can you add to what you have found in the sources? For example:

- You can add to ORGANISATION the work of the ATPUs.
- You can add to PUBLIC OPINION that the Tory (Conservative) government began to worry when it lost local elections.

Plan your answer

- You have identified five factors here – public opinion, peaceful demonstrations, violent protest, organisation and mass passive resistance. You would need to explain the part played by each.
- When historians try to explain why something happened, they think about a web of causation where factors interact. You could do a diagram of how factors interacted to end the poll tax. For example, would millions of people have disobeyed the law without the 'don't pay' campaigns and the protests that brought publicity?
- The question asks if passive resistance was the main factor, so in your answer you should think about the importance of that *and* the other factors.
- Once you have thought about all the sections of your answer, put them in order so that your answer builds up into a convincing explanation. For example, you might decide to write about the most important factor last.

Different people could reach very different conclusions here – and get the same mark! What matters is your explanation and whether you have backed up your ideas with evidence from the sources *and* your own knowledge.

ResultsPlus
Watch out!

The question will always tell you to use the sources and your own knowledge. Every year many students produce excellent answers, but lose marks because they only use the sources or only use their own knowledge. Remember to use both.

Summary

There is not usually a 'right' answer to these judgement questions, but remember to look at both sides of the issue involved and to back up your answer with evidence from the sources and your own knowledge.

Summary: Protest, law and order in the twentieth century

Introduction

The specification requirements for this unit are that you consider the causes, leaders and tactics of protest; the response of the authorities; and the outcome of the protest through four case studies. These four case studies are the two economic protests of the General Strike of 1926 and the miners' strike of 1984–85, and the two political protests of suffragettes 1903–14 and the poll tax protests of 1990.

The following is a list of the key factors concerning the four protests. You need to know:

- the causes of the protest
- the leaders of the protest
- the tactics of the protest
- the response of the authorities
- the outcome of the protest.

Make sure you know these for each of the four case studies. Here are a few quick quiz questions to see how good your knowledge is.

Suffragettes 1903–14

- Who were the NUWSS, who led them and what were their tactics?
- What was the (so-called) 'Cat and Mouse Act', and which suffragette tactic was it a response to?
- When did some women first get the vote, and why do historians debate why they got it?

Who are these women and how influential was their leadership?

General Strike 1926

- Why was the Triple Industrial Alliance formed?
- What problems did the coal industry face before and after the First World War?
- How did the government prepare for the General Strike and how successful were these measures in reducing the scale of the protest?

Who is the character up against the wall, and what was the slogan 'Not a penny off the pay, not a minute on the day' a response to?

Miners' strike 1984–85

- When had the miners last gone on strike prior to 1984 and why had these been such a success?
- Who was Ian MacGregor and what was he asked by the government to do to the mining industry?
- Why were women important in the miners' strike?

Who is the figure in the centre and how significant was his leadership to the way the miners' strike began?

Poll tax protests 1990

- Why did the Conservative Government want to bring in a community charge in the first place?
- When did the poll tax begin in Scotland and when in England and Wales?
- What is an APTU, and when and where was the first one founded?

- Who is this (the man with glasses) and why did poll tax protesters say 'Don't trust this man!'?

Specific factors for protest

Activities

1 The specification for this course lists some specific factors for each protest. Look through the list below, pick a source or information from the coverage in this book or from other resources to show the importance of each specific factor.

2 (a) Think about the factors affecting each protest. Identify the factors that come up again and again: for example, leadership, tactics, government response, public opinion, union support. What else would you add?

  (b) Draw up a table that lists your common factors for the columns and the four protests as the rows.

  (c) Decide the significance of each factor to each protest: you could colour in the table cells red for very significant, orange for fairly significant, yellow for low significance, white for not significant at all.

3 Draw seesaws to represent the balance of power between protesters and government for each of the four protests. Where would you put the balance of power for the suffragettes and the government before the war – for example, a level balance signifying stalemate?

Suffragettes 1903–14: specific factors

- the range of tactics used by the suffragettes
- the difficulties of the authorities in dealing with such tactics.

General Strike 1926: specific factors

- economic situation
- the role of the TUC
- the organisation of resources
- attitudes towards socialism and communism.

Miners' strike 1984–85: specific factors

- economic situation
- government relations with trade unions
- the role of the police.

Poll tax protests 1990: specific factors

- the motives and methods of the poll tax protesters
- the difficulties of the authorities in dealing with violent protest and tax evasion.

KnowZone
Protest, law and order in the twentieth century

Introduction

This unit tests your understanding of the way that a historian uses sources. Because it is important to understand what a source is about and to know about a source's origins and how representative it is of the situation at the time, this work has been set in the context of a series of protests. Your knowledge of these topics will help you to evaluate and use the sources, but you are not expected to have any other knowledge of the protests and you will not get marks for including knowledge in your answers unless it is relevant to the sources.

Checklist (evidence skills)

How well do you think you can do the following?

● Inference: Your ability to work things out from the source. For example, what can you work out about a situation, the attitude of the author, the message of a cartoon, the purpose of a speech?

● Analysis of the source: Which parts of the source create a certain impression? Which parts of a source support or challenge an idea or another source?

● Cross-reference: Checking how far sources agree with each other.

● Evaluation of reliability or usefulness: Using various checks to see how reliable or useful a source is.

● Making a judgement: Weighing up all the evidence for an issue in order to come to a thoughtful and supported conclusion.

Find out more

For more information about the the subjects covered in this section, go to www.heinemann.co.uk/hotlinks (express code 4417P) and click on the appropriate link.

- The BBC website
- The History Learning site
- Spartacus School website
- The Learning curve website

Try to get hold of books such as:

A. Rosen, *Rise Up, Women!*

M. Pugh, *The March of the Women*

A. Raeburn, *The Militant Suffragettes*

For more information about the following, go to www.heinemann.co.uk/hotlinks (express code 4417P) and click on the appropriate link:

- General Strike
- Miners' Strike
- 'Battle of Orgreave'
- The poll tax and opposition to it.

Visit your local library or public record office and see what newspaper reports, leaflets, etc. they have about the resistance to the poll tax that took place in your area or town. If you do this, you might come across some names of local protesters – maybe you could ask your teacher to get them to come to your class to answer questions about the campaign against the poll tax.

Checklist (knowledge of the protests)

How well do you know the following for the suffragettes 1903–14?

- The reasons why the WSPU was set up and who played a leading role in this.
- The early actions of the suffragettes in the years 1903–06.
- The reasons why their actions became more militant after 1906.
- How the Liberal government and the authorities responded to these law-breaking activities.
- Why 'Black Friday' on 18 November 1911 marked a turning-point for WSPU militancy.
- The increasingly violent actions taken by the WSPU after 1912.
- The actions of the WSPU on the outbreak of war in August 1914.

How well do you know the following for the General Strike 1926?

- The reasons why the TIA was set up.
- The early problems of the coal industry and the reasons why these problems became more serious after the First World War.
- How the Conservative government responded to these problems at first.
- Why 1925 marked an important stage in the lead-up to the General Strike.
- What actions the government and the TUC took in the months leading up to the General Strike.
- How the General Strike developed and what the main events were.
- Why the General Strike was called off and what happened immediately afterwards.

How well do you know the following for the miners' strike 1984?

- The earlier problems of the coal industry in the 1970s.
- The reasons why these problems became more serious after 1979.
- The actions taken by the Conservative government and the NUM between 1979 and 1983.
- Why the issue of a national ballot became important at the start and during the course of the strike.
- Why problems between striking miners and the police increasingly led to violence.
- How the miners' strike developed and what the main events were.
- Why the miners' strike was called off in March 1985 and what happened immediately afterwards.

How well do you know the following for the poll tax protests 1990?

- The local government tax the poll tax replaced and the Conservative prime minister strongly associated with this new tax.
- The early resistance to the poll tax in Scotland.
- The various methods used, and the organisations set up, by opponents of the poll tax in England and Wales.
- What happened in London on 31 March 1990 and what impact it had.
- Why and how the poll tax was finally withdrawn.

Student tips

- Try to learn the initials that refer to the main organisations for each protest such as TIA/TUC/OMS for the General Strike – it's the only way to avoid confusion!

- Remember when evaluating sources for reliability/accuracy/usefulness to use the information provided about each source – this will help you to make sensible comments about the nature, origin, purpose of the sources. The information is there for a reason so use it!

Exam questions

This section will give you examples of all of the types of questions you will face in the exam. It will also provide you with student answers and examiner comments to help you understand what to do, and opportunities to write your own answers, which will get you top marks. All the questions will focus on evidence skills, but you will need your knowledge of the topic to help you evaluate the sources. You do not have any choice in the questions in this exam, so you need to make sure that you have covered the whole specification and you are prepared for the sort of question that is asked. The actual exam will probably just focus on one of the protests that you have studied but here we have used examples from each of them.

The first question will test your ability to understand what a source is saying AND to make some valid inferences about it.

The second question will test your ability to understand what a source is saying AND to show how its points are made.

The third question will test your ability to do TWO things:

- to cross-reference two sources to show the extent to which they do and do not support each other

- to comment on the language, content, nature, origin and purpose of those sources.

The fourth question will test your ability to do TWO things:

- to assess the usefulness or reliability of two sources

- to make some judgement about whether one source is more useful and reliable than the other.

The fifth and final type of question is the highest scoring question in the exam. It will test your ability to do TWO things:

- to use both the sources AND your own knowledge to consider a statement or view about an aspect of an historical issue or event

- to come to a BALANCED judgement about the validity of that statement.

ResultsPlus
Maximise your marks

What can you learn from Source A about the aims of the TUC during the General Strike? (6 marks)

Source A: A radio message broadcast by the TUC in May 1926.

> The General Council of the TUC wishes to emphasise the fact that this is an industrial dispute. It expects every member taking part to be exemplary in his conduct and not to give any opportunity for police interference.

Student answer	Examiner comments	Extract from an improved student answer
The source tells us that they expected strikers to behave well to avoid police interference in the strike.	This answer has taken information from the source, but has not made an inference and then supported it with detail from the source which the question requires.	Source A, which is actually from the TUC itself, suggests their main aim during the General Strike is not to give people – and especially the government – any reason to fear the strike. This is why it says 'it wishes to emphasise it is an industrial dispute'. This means that they are saying it is about trying to prevent the pay-cuts and increased working hours being imposed on the miners, not an attempt at revolution. Their aims are also shown by the instruction not to give any excuse for 'police interference'. This is because the TUC wanted to keep it peaceful and so prove that it was not a revolutionary strike.

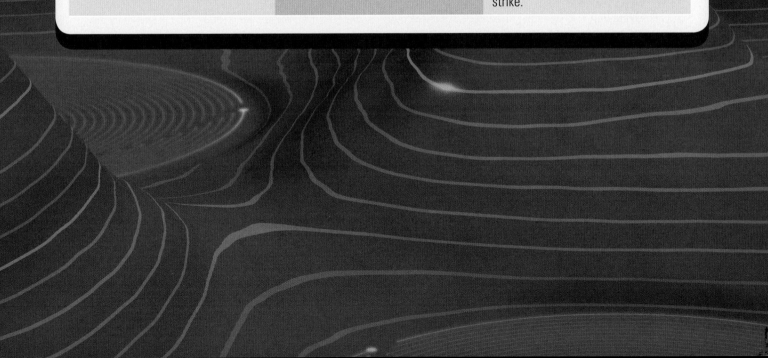

Results Plus
Maximise your marks

How does the artist get his message across in the cartoon in Source B? (8 marks)

Source B: A cartoon produced in 1926 by some of the strikers involved in the General Strike.

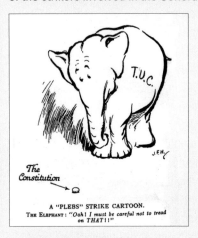

A "PLEBS" STRIKE CARTOON.
THE ELEPHANT: "Ooh! I must be careful not to tread on THAT!!"

Student answer	Examiner comments	Improved student answer
This cartoon shows that although the TUC is big, its leaders are worried about stepping on the constitution. This is saying that TUC leaders were trying not to upset the government.	This answer makes a valid comment about the message of the cartoon (the TUC does not want to anger the government), which is linked to the content of the cartoon, i.e. the TUC is shown as being 'big'. This is enough to get about half marks; however, the student has not really *explained how* the artist has got this message across. To raise this to the top level, the answer should find things in the source that are clearly linked to the message the artist is trying to get across.	The cartoonist seems to be making fun of the TUC leaders – or even attacking them – for being so afraid. It is implying that the TUC should be braver and that the leadership is weak. This is shown by the huge size of the elephant compared with the peanut-sized Constitution. The size is meant to show the increased power of a united trade union movement. The cartoon also gives the message through what the elephant is saying: 'Ooh! I must be careful not to step on THAT!!' In this way the cartoonist gets across the message that in spite of its size and power, the TUC is weak and too fearful to move forward and take action because it is afraid of stepping on (appearing to threaten) the Constitution.

Do you think we can rely on the account given by Pat Rattray in Source C? Explain your answer, using Sources C and D. (10 marks)

Source C: Comments made by Pat Rattray, a striking miner from Fife, Scotland, about the fighting at Orgreave on 18 June 1984.

Source D: Miners running from a police charge at Orgreave on 18 June 1984.

There were thousands of police; we were getting lured into a war, it was like a battle. It was a blisteringly hot day, there were boys up the top sitting about in T-shirts or stripped to the waist, just sunning themselves… it was too quiet so the police sent the horses in, charged us, and smashed miners over the head with their truncheons when they retreated.

Student answer

Source C is from someone who was one of the striking miners at Orgreave on 18 June 1984. He is likely to be sympathetic to the miners and against the police, so he might have deliberately given an anti-police view. Source D, however, is a photograph of the same event, and so must be reliable – this source seems to prove that the account in Source C is probably reliable as it says the same things. So, overall, I think we can rely on the account given in Source C.

Examiner comments

This answer makes some specific and valid comments about the reliability of BOTH the sources mentioned in the question.

This is enough to get about half marks; however, the student has only commented on the origin and nature of the sources. There is nothing precise about the content or possible purpose of the two sources. Nor is there much of an attempt to make a really balanced judgement which weighs up the points about the reliability/unreliability of the two sources before coming to an overall judgement.

To push this up to the top level and so gain full marks, the answer would need to find things in Source C that can and cannot be clearly *linked* to the information provided by Source D to decide how far Source D supports Source C.

After considering these aspects of the content and the nature of BOTH sources it should make a BALANCED judgement.

Improved student answer

Source C is from someone who was one of the striking miners at Orgreave on 18 June 1984, so he is likely to be sympathetic to the miners and against the police. Source D, however, is a photograph of the same event, and shows police charging what is said to be miners. Although it doesn't show mounted police charging, they can be seen at the back. So this seems to confirm Source C when it says 'the police sent in horses, charged us…'. It also shows miners retreating; what could be 'thousands of police'; the miners in shirts, T-shirts or stripped to the waist, just as Source C says. Overall, I think that Source C seems pretty reliable, as much of what it says is supported by Source D. However, Source D is only one photograph. We don't know if the photographer was a miner rather than an impartial journalist. We don't know, either, what happened before this photograph was taken. Importantly, Rattray implies that the police began the violence against peaceful miners. We cannot rely on that part of his account without additional evidence.

KnowZone
Protest, law and order in the twentieth century

ResultsPlus
Maximise your marks

Is Source E more useful than Source F to the historian enquiring about the actions of the police on 'Black Friday', 18 November 1910? Explain your answer, using Sources E and F. (10 marks)

Source E: An extract from an account of 'Black Friday', 18 November 1910, published in the 25 November 1910 edition of the suffragette journal, *Votes for Women*.

Source F: A photograph of a suffragette struggling with a policeman on 'Black Friday', 18 November 1910.

> On learning that Mr. Asquith had shelved the Conciliation Bill it was decided to send a deputation to him. This deputation consisted of over 300 women. The treatment, which this deputation received, was the worst that has been meted out to any deputation since the conflict between women and the Government began. The orders of the Home Secretary were, apparently, that the police were to be present both in uniform and also in plain clothes among the crowd and that the women were to be thrown from one to the other. As a result, many women were severely hurt, and several were knocked down and bruised. Finally, one hundred and fifteen women were arrested.

Student answer

Source E is useful to an extent, as it tells us that there were large numbers of women involved in the protest on 18 November 1910, and that the government had ordered uniformed police to be present. This source also tells us that struggles between the police and the protesters took place, and that many women were injured.
Source F is also useful as it shows a suffragette struggling with a policeman and that there was a large number of other policemen present. It doesn't show any of the serious violence mentioned by Source E.

Examiner comments

This answer makes some specific and valid comments about the utility/usefulness of BOTH the sources mentioned in the question.
The student has focused on the content of the two sources and has done enough to get about half marks. However, the student has not commented on the nature, origin, purpose or typicality of the sources. To push this up to the top level and so gain full marks, all these issues would need to be addressed.

Extract from an improved student answer

Source F is useful to show us the action of this policeman at this moment, and also that there are a few policemen involved, but we cannot from this judge the extent of any violence used, although the suffragette is being pulled away from the railing. Source E gives us a great deal more information, but all of it has been chosen for publication in *Votes for Women*. The journal may be seeking to stir up anger at the way the police treated the deputation so that it can increase support for the movement. However, I think Source E is more useful as it gives some precise details which the historian could then check up on.

Do you think that the public protests and demonstrations used by anti-poll tax protesters were the most effective way of resisting the tax? Explain your answer, using your own knowledge, and Sources G, H and I. (16 marks)

Source G: Comments made by Neil Kinnock, the leader of the Labour Party, following anti-poll tax demonstrations outside several town halls. Printed in *The Guardian*, 10 March 1990.

> [People do not deserve to be] exploited by Toy Town revolutionaries who pretend that the tax can be stopped and the government toppled simply by non-payment.

Source H: An anti-poll tax protester.

Source I: Anti-poll tax protesters burning their poll tax bills.

Student answer

I do not think that the protests and demonstrations were the most effective way of resisting the tax. This is because the media, many members of the public and leaders of the opposition parties opposed the violence, which often took place during the demonstrations. Such scenes lost the campaign a lot of support, which could have been useful.

This was especially true of the national demonstration, on 31 March 1990. This ended in a serious riot in which buildings were burned, and many police and protesters were injured. Much more effective were the various methods used to avoid payment and to resist the attempts of councils to collect it. The local Anti-Poll Tax Unions gave useful advice to local communities by issuing guides and leaflets which explained to people what to do.

As a result, hundreds of thousands refused to register or to pay. Then, when bailiffs tried to seize goods to the value of the tax owed, local groups helped people to prevent the bailiffs from gaining entry to homes. By the time that the tax was abolished, it was said that 17.5 million people had either not paid or were in serious arrears.

Examiner comments

This answer gives some precise own knowledge and is focused on the question. However, the answer has some significant weaknesses: it is unbalanced, in that, although it makes a judgement, it has nothing positive to say about the public protests; AND it makes NO reference to any of the sources. As a result of the lack of any reference to a single source, this answer cannot be awarded higher than level 2 (5–8 marks). To push this up to the top level and so gain full marks, these aspects would all need to be addressed, making sure that precise references are made to all three sources to show how they do AND do not support the view raised in the question.

Extract from an improved student answer

The public protests and demonstrations used by anti-poll tax protesters were mostly an effective way of resisting the tax. Although violence did break out on some of them. Especially important were protests such as those shown in Source I, where people burnt their bills in public. Also, the violence of the police on the national demonstration worried many people and gained some support for the cause.

However, it is true that the violence – or the way it was reported in the media – lost the support of many members of the public.

The most effective ways of resisting the tax were undoubtedly non-registration, non-payment and attempts to prevent councils from collecting it. It was this non-payment rather than public protests that led to it being replaced by a new community charge. Although the protests played an important part in encouraging people to break, and to keep breaking, the law by not paying the tax, it was the non-payment itself which proved the most effective way of resisting the tax.

Welcome to exam zone

Revising for your exams can be a daunting prospect. In this part of the book we'll take you through the best way of revising for your exams, step by step, to ensure you get the best results possible.

Zone In!

Have you ever become so absorbed in a task that suddenly it feels entirely natural and easy to perform? This is a feeling familiar to many athletes and performers. They work hard to recreate it in competition in order to do their very best. It's a feeling of being 'in the zone', and if you can achieve that same feeling in an examination, the chances are you'll perform brilliantly.

The good news is that you can get 'in the zone' by taking some simple steps in advance of the exam. Here are our top tips.

UNDERSTAND IT
Make sure you understand the exam process and what revision you need to do. This will give you confidence and also help you to get things into proportion. These pages are a good place to find some starting pointers for performing well in exams.

FRIENDS AND FAMILY

Make sure that your friends and family know when you want to revise. Even share your revision plan with them. Learn to control your times with them, so you don't get distracted. This means you can have better quality time with them when you aren't revising, because you aren't worrying about what you ought to be doing.

DEAL WITH DISTRACTIONS

Think about the issues in your life that may interfere with revision. Write them all down. Then think about how you can deal with each so they don't affect your revision.

COMPARTMENTALISE

You might not be able to deal with all the issues that can distract you. For example, you may be worried about a friend who is ill, or just be afraid of the exam. In this case, there is still a useful technique you can use. Put all of these worries into an imagined box in your mind at the start of your revision (or in the exam) and mentally lock it. Only open it again at the end of your revision session (or exam).

DIET AND EXERCISE

Make sure you eat sensibly and exercise as well! If your body is not in the right state, how can your mind be? A substantial breakfast will set you up for the day, and a light evening meal will keep your energy levels high.

BUILD CONFIDENCE
Use your revision time not only to revise content, but also to build your confidence in readiness for tackling the examination. For example, try tackling a short sequence of easy tasks in record time.

Planning Zone

The key to success in exams and revision often lies in good planning. Knowing **what** you need to do and **when** you need to do it is your best path to a stress-free experience. Here are some top tips in creating a great personal revision plan.

First of all, **know your strengths and weaknesses**.

Go through each topic making a list of how well you think you know the topic. Use your mock examination results and/or any other test results that are available as a check on your self-assessment. This will help you to plan your personal revision effectively, putting extra time into your weaker areas.

Next, *create your plan!*
Remember to make time for considering how topics interrelate.

For example, in History you will be expected to know not just the date when an event happened, but why it happened, how important it was, and how one event relates to another.

The specification quite clearly states when you are expected to be able to link one topic to another so plan this into your revision sessions.

You will be tested on this in the exam and you can gain valuable marks by showing your ability to do this.

Finally, *follow the plan!*
You can use the revision sections in the following pages to kick-start your revision.

163

MAY

SUNDAY	MONDAY	TUES
30	30	1

Be realistic about how much time you can devote to your revision, but also make sure you put in enough time. Give yourself regular breaks or different activities to give your life some variance. Revision need not be a prison sentence!

Find out your exam dates. Go to the Edexcel website to find all final exam dates, and check with your teacher.

iew Secti
complete t
ractice ex
question

Chunk your revision in each subject down into smaller sections. This will make it more manageable and less daunting.

Draw up a list of all the dates from the start of your revision right through to your exams.

13

Review Sectio
Complete three
practice exam

20

Review Sectio
Try the Keywor
Quiz again

Make sure you allow time for assessing your progress against your initial self-assessment. Measuring progress will allow you to see and be encouraged by your improvement. These little victories will build your confidence.

22

EXAM DAY!

27

28

29

Don't Panic Zone

As you get close to completing your revision, the Big Day will be getting nearer and nearer. Many students find this the most stressful time and tend to go into panic mode, either working long hours without really giving their brains a chance to absorb information or giving up and staring blankly at the wall.

Panicking simply makes your brain seize up and you find that information and thoughts simply cannot flow naturally. You become distracted and anxious, and things seem worse than they are. Many students build the exams up into more than they are. Remember: the exams are not trying to catch you out! If you have studied the course, there will be no surprises on the exam paper!

Student tip

I know how silly it is to panic, especially if you've done the work and know your stuff. I was asked by a teacher to produce a report on a project I'd done, and I panicked so much I spent the whole afternoon crying and worrying. I asked other people for help, but they were panicking too. In the end, I calmed down and looked at the task again. It turned out to be quite straightforward and, in the end, I got my report finished first and it was the best of them all!

In the exam you don't have much time, so you can't waste it by panicking. The best way to control panic is simply to do what you have to do. Think carefully for a few minutes, then start writing and as you do, the panic will drain away.

Don't panic

ExamZone

For the **Crime and punishment** paper, you will have an hour and a quarter for the exam, and in that time you have to answer four questions. You need to answer Questions 1 and 2. Then you must choose to answer one question from Questions 3 and 4, and then choose to answer one question from Questions 5 and 6. You must answer both part (a) and (b) of the question you choose.

For the **Protest, law and order** paper, you will have an hour and a quarter and in that time you have to answer five questions. There are no choices for this exam.

The questions on the paper are worth different numbers of marks and it is important that you use your time effectively. Don't waste precious time on a 4-mark question that might then leave you with too little time to spend on a question which is worth 16 marks!

Meet the exam paper

This diagram shows the front cover of the exam paper. These instructions, information and advice will always appear on the front of the paper. It is worth reading it carefully now. Check you understand it. Now is a good opportunity to ask your teacher about anything you are not sure of here.

Print your surname here, and your other names afterwards. This is an additional safeguard to ensure that the exam board awards the marks to the right candidate.

Here you fill in the school's exam number.

Ensure that you understand exactly how long the examination will last, and plan your time accordingly.

Note that the quality of your written communication will also be marked. Take particular care to present your thoughts and work at the highest standard you can, for maximum marks.

Here you fill in your personal exam number. Take care when writing it down because the number is important to the exam board when writing your score.

In this box, the examiner will write the total marks you have achieved in the exam paper.

Make sure that you understand exactly which questions from which sections you should attempt.

Don't feel that you have to fill the answer space provided. Everybody's handwriting varies, so a long answer from you may take up as much space a short answer from someone else.

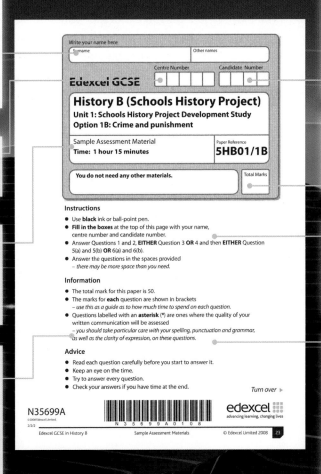

Understanding the language of the exam paper

Describe	The examiner is looking for a concise and organised account. Jot down three or four points in the margin that you want to include in your answer. Arrange them in the most logical order.
Explain how	The examiner is trying to discover whether you understand the key ideas about how and why developments happened in the history of crime and punishment. The more detail you can give, the more marks you will receive.
Give reasons for your answer	You need to provide an explanation.
How far	The examiner is looking for points for and against the statement. Make sure you find some on both sides.
Do you agree?	You are free to agree or disagree. What makes a difference is how well you back up your case.

ZoneOut

This section provides answers to the most common questions students have about what happens after they complete their exams. For more information, visit www.heinemann.co.uk/hotlinks (express code 4417P) and click on ExamZone.

About your grades

Whether you've done better than, worse than, or just as you expected, your grades are the final measure of your performance on your course and in the exams. On this page we explain some of the information that appears on your results slip and tell you what to do if you think something is wrong. We answer the most common questions about grades and look at some of the options facing you.

When will my results be published?

Results for summer examinations are issued on the **middle** two Thursdays in August, with GCE first and GCSE second.

Can I get my results online?

Visit www.heinemann.co.uk/hotlinks (express code 4417P) and click on Results Plus, where you will find detailed student results information including the 'Edexcel Gradeometer' which demonstrates how close you were to the nearest grade boundary. You will need a password to access this information, which can be retrieved from your school's exam secretary.

I haven't done as well as I expected. What can I do now?

First of all, talk to your subject teacher. After all the teaching that you have had, tests and internal examinations, he/she is the person who best knows what grade you are capable of achieving. Take your results slip to your subject teacher, and go through the information on it in detail. If you both think there is something wrong with the result, the school or college can apply to see your completed examination paper and then, if necessary, ask for a re-mark immediately. The original mark can be confirmed or lowered, as well as raised, as a result of a re-mark.

How do my grades compare with those of everybody else who sat this exam?

You can compare your results with those of others in the UK who have completed the same examination using the information on Edexcel website at www.heinemann.co.uk/hotlinks (express code 4417P) by clicking on Edexcel.

I achieved a higher mark for the same unit last time. Can I use that result?

Yes. The higher score is the one that goes towards your overall grade. The best result will be used automatically when the overall grade is calculated. You do not need to ask the exam board to take into account a previous result. This will be done automatically so you can be assured that all your best unit results have gone into calculating your overall grade.

What happens if I was ill over the period of my examinations?

If you become ill before or during the examination period you are eligible for special consideration. This also applies if you have been affected by an accident, bereavement or serious disturbance during an examination.

If my school has requested special consideration for me, is this shown on my Statement of Results?

If your school has requested special consideration for you, it is not shown on your results slip, but it will be shown on a subject mark report that is sent to your school or college. If you want to know whether special consideration was requested for you, you should ask your Examinations Officer.

Can I have a re-mark of my examination paper?

Yes, this is possible, but remember that only your school or college can apply for a re-mark, not you or your parents/carers. First of all, you should consider carefully whether or not to ask your school or college to make a request for a re-mark. It is worth knowing that very few re-marks result in a change to a grade – not because Edexcel is embarrassed that a change of marks has been made, but simply because a re-mark request has shown that the original marking was accurate. Check the closing date for re-marking requests with your Examinations Officer.

When I asked for a re-mark of my paper, my subject grade went down. What can I do?

There is no guarantee that your grades will go up if your papers are re-marked. They can also go down or stay the same. After a re-mark, the only way to improve your grade is to take the examination again. Your school or college Examinations Officer can tell you when you can do that.

How many times can I re-sit a unit?

You can resit a unit from your History B course once and the best result for each unit in the course will then count towards the final grade. If you have finished all your assessments for the course and then decide you want to resit a unit, you have to do a minimum of 40 per cent of the assessments again in your resit.

For much more information, go to www.heinemann.co.uk/hotlinks (express code 4417P) and click on ExamZone.

Glossary

This Glossary contains all the key word definitions, plus some other terms used in the book that may be unfamiliar to you.

Assize – A court that sat at intervals in each county of England and Wales, presided over by judges who travelled from place to place.

Capital offence – A **crime** punishable by the death penalty.

Capital punishment – Execution of those found guilty of **crimes** that carry the death penalty.

Citizen – An inhabitant of a town or city, especially one entitled to the rights of a freeman or woman.

Civil disobedience – Refusal to obey government demands or commands.

Community – A body of people living in the same area.

Conscientious objector – A person refusing **conscription** to fight in a war on moral, religious or political grounds.

Conscription – Forcing people to join the military.

Crime – An act that is made illegal by laws passed by parliament.

Democracy – A system in which leaders of a government are elected by the adult citizens, or where members of an organisation have a say in the organisation's activities.

Demonstration – A public protest.

Deterrence – Discouraging **crime** by using harsh **punishments** to frighten people.

Domestic violence – Violence in the home.

Enforcement – Putting law into force; making sure that everyone obeys the law.

Evil spirits – Forces thought to be those of the devil.

Extremist – A person who is willing to use violence to further a cause.

Familiar – An animal given to a witch by the devil, to assist them in their work.

Force-feeding – Using force to make hunger strikers eat; liquid food is poured through a tube into the stomach.

Heresy – Holding religious beliefs that are different from the official religion enforced by the authorities; the people concerned were called heretics.

Homicide – Another term for murder or manslaughter.

Hunger strike – Refusing to eat, in order to make a political point or further a cause.

Industrialisation – The growth in numbers of factories and the related expansion of towns in the 18th-and 19th-centuries.

Inflation – Rising prices, especially when prices go up more than wages.

Jury – A group of people who decide on a person's guilt or innocence, usually in a court.

Justice of the Peace – An unpaid judge who presides over cases involving less serious **crimes**.

King's peace – Protection offered to **citizens** by the monarch.

Laws – Rules made by parliament that must be obeyed by the **citizens** of a country.

Militant – Prepared to take dramatic, or violent, action in support of a cause.

Misogyny – Dislike of women.

Mutiny – **Rebellion** in the military services.

Non-combatant – Not engaged in fighting during a war.

Ordeal – A test of guilt or innocence involving pain and an appeal for a sign from God.

Over-mighty subject – A person whose power threatens the monarch.

Pacifism – Belief that violence is always wrong.

Petition – A list of signatures of people supporting a cause, with the intention of changing the minds of those in government.

Picket – A group of workers on **strike** who stand outside a workplace and try to persuade others not to enter; flying pickets are those who travel to other workplaces to encourage more support.

Policing – **Enforcement** of the law and catching criminals.

Posse – A group of citizens helping a sheriff or constable catch a suspected criminal.

Possession – Being controlled by an **evil spirit**.

Prevention – Putting measures in place to stop **crimes** being committed, e.g. by using burglar alarms or by solving social problems.

Pricking – Sticking a needle all over a person's body to find out if that person is a witch.

Propaganda – Information, especially biased or misleading, that is used to promote a political cause.

Property crime – **Crime** against objects and possessions, not people.

Punishment – Inflicting a penalty on someone who has committed a **crime**.

Rebellion – Rising up against a ruler; defiance of authority.

Reform – Changing things for the better.

Rehabilitation – Making someone fit to lead a better life and earn a living after imprisonment.

Retribution – Literally, giving back; another word for punishment.

Scab – An insulting term for a person who works while others from the same industry or factory are on **strike**, or who is brought in by employers to break a strike.

Separate System – In prisons, a system where each prisoner was kept in a separate cell and had almost no contact with others.

Silent System – In prisons, the performing of activities in silence.

Solidarity – When people with the same interests and aims join together to support each other, e.g. in a **strike** or protest.

Strike – To refuse to work, in order to put pressure on employers or government.

Suffrage – The right to vote.

Swimming test – Test to see if a person was a witch by throwing them in a pond or river; if the person sank, this was a sign of innocence.

Technology – The use of scientific knowledge for practical purposes, e.g. using computers to solve **crimes**.

Treason – Betraying one's country, especially by trying to overthrow the government or kill the monarch.

Tribunal – A type of court; a panel of people brought together to settle certain types of dispute, or to judge certain types of **crime**, e.g. in the military.

Women's refuge – A place where women who have escaped violence in their homes can find safety.

Index

In the following index, main entries of key words are given in **bold** type. For definitions of these, as well as some more definitions of unfamiliar words, see the Glossary on pages 168–69.